MW00446025

EMOTIONAL INTELLIGENCE
GAME CHANGERS:

101 Simple Ways to Win at Work + Life

BY HARVEY DEUTSCHENDORF

Dedication

This book is dedicated to those who continue pushing their comfort zones, keep learning, growing, and moving toward their dreams and passions. Despite obstacles and hardships along the way, they will in the end know that they gave it their best and will have the peace of not knowing regret.

Dexterity, LLC
604 Magnolia Lane
Nashville, TN 37211

Printed in Canada.

First edition: 2023
10 9 8 7 6 5 4 3 2 1

ISBN: 978-1-947297-69-2 (Hardcover)
ISBN: 978-1-947297-70-8 (E-book)

Publisher's Cataloging-in-Publication Data

Names: Deutschendorf, Harvey, author. | Freedman, Joshua, foreword author.
Title: Emotional intelligence game changers : 101 simple ways to win at work + life / by Harvey Deutschendorf; foreword by Joshua Freedman.
Description: Includes bibliographical references. | Nashville, TN: Dexterity, 2023.
Identifiers: ISBN: 978-1-947297-69-2 (hardcover) | 9781947297708 (ebook)
Subjects: LCSH Emotional intelligence. | Emotions and cognition. | Leadership.
| Success. | Success in business. | Self-help. | BISAC Business & Economics /
Leadership | Self-Help / Personal Growth / Success
Classification: LCC BF576 .D48 2023 | DDC 152.4 --dc23

Cover design by Thinkpen Design
Interior design by PerfecType, Nashville, TN

Table of Contents

iv   TABLE OF CONTENTS

Foreword

I n these unprecedented times . . ."
After the roller coaster of recent years, how tired are you of that
phrase? Yet research is increasingly clear: there is no "new normal"; we're living in an era of accelerating complexity. Which
means it's time for real leaders to step up. It's easy to "be a leader"
when everything is going well. But during times like today, we see
who's committed to growing themselves and their people to succeed through challenges.

What does that kind of leadership demand?

Once, all someone needed to stand out as a leader was a little
extra know-how—an edge that allowed them to stand out above
the norm. Now that AI knows more than people, knowledge
holds little value. Yet people still need leaders. In my research,
what differentiates high-performing leaders today is a radically
different set of skills. It's all about people.

Today, "better leaders" means "better people people"—people
who "get it" quickly, who engage others and bring them into align-
ment. Your challenge isn't about knowing; it's about engaging.
Fostering collaboration across boundaries. Galvanizing your own
vision and energy such that you can enroll people from diverse
backgrounds and support them to go beyond what was possible
without you.

The organization I lead, Six Seconds, works in 200 countries
and territories. We're on a mission to increase the world's emotional intelligence. We measure these skills in all sectors, and the
bad news is: most aspects of emotional intelligence are actually
declining. The good news is: people with these skills stand out.

Even better news: you have this book to help you do just that. So many leadership books are filled with vague theories and "things to know." Here you have something much more valuable. Since the earliest writings on emotional intelligence, it's bothered me that the theories are often detached from the real world. Harvey's writing is the opposite. Here you'll find practical, actionable tips that will make a difference.

To combat an overly academic approach, I've advocated a radically simple definition of emotional intelligence: *being smarter with feelings*. We all have emotions; they're part of basic human biology and part of how we're wired to assess risks and seek opportunities. We can ignore the insights of emotions, but that's dumb. We can overindulge in emotions, and that's also a mistake. The middle ground, however, unleashes phenomenal power.

How do you use emotional intelligence? At Six Seconds, we support a three-step process. In this book, you'll find numerous, specific tips to further flesh that out, but here are our basic steps:

1. *Leaders go first.* To actually grow and practice these skills, you must start with a greater awareness of your emotions.
2. *Become more intentional about your own responses.* Shift from reaction to response both in your own interactions and in the organizational systems you build.
3. *Put that awareness and intentionality into service of something worthwhile.* Become a leader worth following by connecting with others at a deeper level and connecting with purpose.

That's it. Put those three steps into action—make it a practice. Make it part of who you are as a leader, and you'll see dramatic shifts in yourself, your team, and your enterprise. Plus, you'll be part of our vision at Six Seconds: a billion people practicing emotional intelligence. Just imagine a world where everyone was showing up like this. Aware. Intentional. Purposeful. That would make our lives, our workplaces/schools/communities, and our world a better place. Let's go!

Joshua Freedman
Cofounder & CEO, Six Seconds - The Emotional Intelligence Network | Author of *At the Heart of Leadership*

Introduction

The ancient Greeks were quite aware of the power of emotions. "Any one can get angry—that is easy," Aristotle wrote in *Nicomachean Ethics, Book 2;* "but to do this to the right person, to the right extent, at the right time, with the right motive, and in the right way, that is not for every one, nor is it easy."

Aristotle nailed the challenge of *emotional intelligence*—the skill of understanding and channeling our emotions, rather than letting them control us. Several thousand years later, humans began understanding how to define emotional intelligence, quantify it, assess it, and come up with ways to develop it.

Emotional intelligence, or lack thereof, impacts all of us from an early age. My father was an angry man, and we were constantly afraid and on guard of his anger boiling over. Poorly educated, my father saw little opportunity for meaningful work in Europe and was drawn to the idea of going to Canada to start his own business. Penniless and close to middle-aged, he and my mother set out for a new beginning.

Isolated from anyone we knew and starting from scratch—I believe those factors contributed to the abusive, dysfunctional family dynamics that later played out. However, while my father showed the poor emotional intelligence described by Aristotle, my mother was the opposite: patient, loving, and kind. I clearly saw what it means when someone practices being emotionally intelligent and what it looks like when one does not.

As I grew up, graduating from university and starting out in the real world, I was guarded, suspicious, and fearful of criticism. This unhealthy attitude spilled over into every aspect of my life.

Unable to share what I was feeling, I withdrew and began creating the same environment that caused my father to lash out in anger. At work I was known to be aloof and distant though I produced high quality work. Overall, I lacked people skills and wasn't a team player. I was in a rut, and I didn't know how to break free.

Then one day I heard of a new book called *Emotional Intelligence: Why It Can Matter More than IQ*, by Daniel Goleman. I picked up a copy. A line from the book jumped out at me: "Intelligence can come to naught when emotions hold sway."

That was my aha moment. I knew I had discovered something that would profoundly change my life.

After reading Goleman's book, I read every book and article that I could find on the subject and listened to experts constantly. In 1997 I left the tourism industry and joined Alberta Human Resources, whose mandate was to help chronically unemployed people maintain work. It was a perfect place to continue growing my emotional intelligence skills while helping others grow theirs. I began speaking to groups on EI, and by 2000, I became certified to administer the BarOn EQI Assessment tool and joined the Mankind Project, a men's organization that provides men a safe place to share their emotions and work through any emotional roadblocks holding them back.

As I grew in awareness and understanding of my emotions, my work life changed for the positive. Previously, I was wary and defensive, always suspicious that others would take credit for my work. But with the emotional intelligence work I was putting in, my trust grew, and I looked for ways to help with extra projects and speak positively about my coworkers during meetings. I reached out to colleagues and supervisors and got to know them on a personal level. Soon I was getting those promotions I used to be passed up for, an indication that I had changed and could move on from the negative behaviors I used to be known for at work. It wasn't long before I actually started to enjoy going to work.

While the changes for me at work were welcome, I saw the greatest benefit in my personal relationships. Becoming more open, transparent, and empathic made me someone whom others wanted to be around. As my walls came down and confidence grew, I formed close, lasting relationships with people I respected and looked up to. For the first time in my life, I felt true happiness, and the future looked promising.

Since then, I wrote *The Other Kind of Smart: Simple Ways to Boost Your Emotional Intelligence for Greater Personal Effectiveness and Success*, which was published in 2009 in multiple countries. I've continued to teach, speak, and write on emotional intelligence for more than twenty years.

Emotional intelligence is more than a theory that determines how we humans turn out; It can be the backbone of happier and healthier lives. Without it we run the risk of never improving, growing, or making meaningful, lasting connections. These principles guide us toward full, rewarding, and productive lives—lives worth living.

With today's rapid pace of change, exponential increases in technology, and shortening of attention spans, we often find ourselves looking for quicker answers and solutions. With that in mind, I've written 101 simple tips on how and why it is important to be emotionally intelligent. Giving actionable steps and solid advice, I lay out the principles that have helped me in my own life as well as the best advice I've learned from others. My book is written for those of any age and background, and I've organized it so you can jump in at any chapter and read the tip that applies most to what you're going through. As you read, I hope you find the importance of emotional intelligence too and at the very least, I hope you discover practical advice for the moment.

TIP 1

Develop self-awareness

Self-awareness is the keystone of emotional intelligence, according to Daniel Goleman, author of Emotional Intelligence: Why It Can Matter More than IQ.

Before we can make changes in ourselves, we need to know who we are now. The Dalai Lama summed it up when he said, "To have greater self-awareness or understanding means to have a better grasp of reality." While self-awareness lies at the root of emotional intelligence, acquiring it is a lifelong journey. Here are several actions you, as a leader, can take to develop your self-awareness.

- **Write down your emotions**

While it is difficult to remember all the emotions you went through during the day, writing them down is helpful. Chris Kneeland, CEO of advisory firm Cult Collective, said he always used to say "I think" instead of "I feel." He continued, "Just giving myself permission to acknowledge my emotions and accept that feelings are as important as knowledge was a big step for me."

● Become aware of what triggers you and why

We are constantly being triggered, but often it goes under our radar. Perhaps someone or something you have a strong reaction to reminds you of past persons or events. Dr. Rick Brandon, author of *Straight Talk: Influence Skills for Collaboration and Commitment*, recommends whenever you are triggered, you stop to examine your "self-talk"—that little voice in your head that programs your brain. Remember: as with any programming, it's garbage in, garbage out.

● Avoid making judgments about emotions

We can feel guilty for having what we consider bad emotions. However, emotions are neither good nor bad; they are just giving us information. What we do with them is what matters. Try to understand what your emotions are telling you without making any judgment about them.

● Feel the discomfort and do it anyway

It may be difficult to look at your emotions because that action can produce many levels of discomfort. If this happens, recognize that you are doing important work and that this kind of work is not easy.

● Check how you show up physically

How do you show up physically when you are experiencing strong emotions? Have a look in the mirror and see if you can spot your emotions as reflected in your face and body posture. Is there a connection between your physical appearance and how you feel?

- Increase your feelings vocabulary

Even though we have many and various levels of emotion, we are usually only conscious of a few. Tools like Plutchik's wheel of emotions will help expand your awareness. Recognizing an emotion and saying it out loud brings it clearly into your consciousness and helps you to manage that emotion more effectively.

EI Exercise:

Spend time in reflection. Imagine looking at yourself from the outside and witnessing your emotions, thoughts, and behaviors. Notice how you respond to events. Realizing that you have the ability to choose your response at any time is a powerful step in your emotional growth process.

TIP 2

Boost your emotional intelligence

People don't leave their jobs; they leave their bosses.

Years ago, people were promoted based on their knowledge and skills. Little thought was given to their ability to develop strong relationships with others in order to work effectively with them. Some call this people skills, soft skills, or emotional intelligence. No matter the term, the ability to communicate and motivate others has become a skill set increasingly sought in leadership positions. Hiring and developing this in leaders is crucial to the long-term success of any organization. Here are seven reasons for leaders to boost their emotional intelligence.

● Increase self-awareness

Being aware of our emotions, how they affect us, and how we come across to others is crucial for any healthy relationship. Strong leaders will continue to develop themselves and be open to feedback—exhibiting vulnerability when called for. This increases their ability to connect with others, build trust, and get the most from everyone around them.

• Build effective relationships with others

Most successful leaders work hard to overcome personal bias, inflated egos, and self-focus. Instead of taking things personally, emotionally intelligent leaders work to see things from the other person's perspective, allowing them to build the type of relationships that make people feel valued and appreciated, and want to stay.

• Increase communication and listening skills

Many people complain that they are not heard and listened to in their workplace. In conversations, instead of listening closely for understanding, many try to think of a response. In contrast, strong leaders listen to those around them and let them know that they are heard, that their opinions and ideas are valued. Leaders with high emotional intelligence are aware of the impact of their words, tone of voice, and body language.

• Increase empathy

The ability to understand others and empathize with them might well be the most important leadership skill. People are constantly challenged by highly stressful situations, both at work and outside. Death, illness in the family, divorce and relationship breakups, and many other events significantly affect our ability to function at work. Leaders strong in empathy are able to recognize and effectively navigate these situations that call for a caring support of their people while at the same time minimizing disruption at the organization. During difficult times, empathic leaders can make the difference between a valued employee bonding more closely with the organization or deciding it is time to move on.

- Build teamwork and cooperation

Strong leaders smooth out and overcome the inevitable conflicts that arise when a group of people work together. They look for opportunities to encourage and praise others in the organization for their successes. More importantly, leaders know how to respond when things aren't going well. They look for solutions and lessons instead of apportioning blame. Excellent leaders also promote collaboration.

- Model healthy emotional management

Leaders who manage their emotions set a healthy and positive example for the organization. They connect and build positive relationships, setting a standard for others to emulate. This builds trust and creates a positive image of the company as a great place to work.

- Articulate a shared vision for the organization

A healthy workplace spends less time on conflict, backstabbing, and destructive politics, thus freeing up energy toward shared goals. Leaders who articulate a vision that is shared by everyone will spend more time on the work needed to grow the organization. When everyone is driven by a shared cause, there is no need for micromanagement. Employees will feel empowered to use their talents and gifts toward the united goal.

EI Exercise:

While beneficial, it is not expected that you would read this book straight through, front to back. Instead, the format encourages you to find topics of immediate interest.

As you will see, many of the same traits of emotional intelligence come into play regardless of the subject matter. Such repetition serves to reinforce those traits, embedding them in the fabric of your being. Whenever possible, I encourage you to work on the EI Exercise found at the end of every entry. So here's your assignment: browse the table of contents, select and study the tip that catches your attention—and continue on your path to greater emotional intelligence.

TIP 3

Hone the art of influencing others

"I've learned that people will forget what you said, people will forget what you did, but people will never forget how you made them feel." —Maya Angelou, poet and civil rights activist

Real influence rarely comes from title or position. It comes from understanding people and their deepest, most fundamental wants and needs. Everyone at some level wants to be heard, understood, and appreciated. By understanding these basic needs, and keeping them in mind when dealing with others, you can increase your influence. Here are several ways to do so.

● **Develop listening abilities**

Whether or not you agree with someone, everyone has a need to be heard. That means you must carefully listen. Most people are busy thinking of a response, a rebuttal, or what they want to talk about instead of actively paying attention. One way of increasing listening skills is to repeat in your own words what someone just said. If you're not clear, ask questions. Good listening requires us to overcome the urge to think ahead to what we want to say and stay focused on the person speaking.

● **Follow nonverbal cues**

When two people are intensely connected in conversation they tend to model each other's nonverbal cues such as smiling, moving toward the other, and making eye contact. But we can also make a conscious effort to model these cues; and when we do so, the person we are speaking with becomes even more open to our ideas. Their comfort level increases when they feel that we get them.

● **Recognize the accomplishments of others**

Everyone appreciates being acknowledged for something they did well and have pride in. Acknowledging those accomplishments with sincerity will ensure that you will be remembered in a positive vein—putting you in a category above all the people who haven't seemed to notice.

● **Ask for advice from others**

Everyone has an area of knowledge or expertise they are proud of, and asking them to share it gives their confidence a boost. This also raises your status level in their mind—again, you are someone who recognizes the value of what they have to offer.

● **Say their name and remember important details about them**

Perhaps the most beautiful word is the sound of our own name. Remembering someone's name and greeting them with it is influence 101. If someone remembers our name, it means we have made an impression, and that person made the effort to remember. The more significant information you can remember about people, the stronger impression you will make and the more influential you will become.

- **Look for common ground**

Regardless of our differences, we can find something we share with virtually anyone. When we uncover that commonality, we can develop stronger connections and greater influence. In preparation for meeting with someone, try to discern an area of common interest. You'll get the conversation off to a positive start and flowing in the right direction.

EI Exercise:

Have trouble remembering names? In a small notebook, keep a running tab of the names of people you've met and a key detail or two of the meeting. Review your list often.

TIP 4

Shrug off imposter syndrome

Actor Jodie Foster, after receiving an Oscar for best actress in The Accused, *said she feared someone would come to her home and tell her she had been awarded the prize by mistake.*

After pushing through your comfort zone, struggling, and persisting in your career goals, you finally arrive. You've accomplished something of great significance, something rewarding and desirable. By all accounts you should feel fantastic, on top of the world! Instead, you have a strange feeling that you don't belong, that you will be found out and everyone will know you are a fraud. This is called "imposter syndrome," and you are far from alone in this feeling. Many well-known, successful people from all walks of life have experienced the same. So how do you tame the monster whispering in your mind that you aren't for real? Use these techniques to slay this beast of negativity.

- **Share your feelings with those you know will be supportive**

Naming your fear—talking about it with those you trust—helps lessen the syndrome's grip. Often these individuals will share similar experiences. They can also give you feedback on your capabilities and their positive perceptions of you.

- **Resist comparing yourself to others**

Comparing yourself to others is a futile exercise. There will always be people who are ahead of you and behind you. Everyone's journey is different and yours is uniquely yours. Instead of looking at someone else's accomplishments, focus on how far you've come and strive for continuous improvement over your former self.

- **Don't take yourself too seriously**

Writer and artist Elbert Hubbard, known for his pithy wit, once said, "Do not take yourself too seriously. You will never get out of it alive!" A great sense of humor and the ability to laugh at ourselves make everything in life go more smoothly. They help prevent us from feeling overwhelmed by our achievements and keep our disappointments in perspective.

- **Remind yourself that no one is perfect**

Perfectionists set themselves up for continuous frustration because they will never be able to master this unachievable level. Look at life as a journey with ups and downs, successes and failures. Remind yourself that even the most successful people have failed at some point in their lives, often numerous times. Strive to be gentle with yourself and surround yourself with people who are gentle as well. Consider a "failure" as a learning opportunity, and you're less likely to repeat the error.

EI Exercise:

Keep a running file of your accomplishments—a resume of life achievements. Additionally, consider placing any examples of your wins (diplomas, certificates, letters of recommendation, awards, etc.) in plain sight so you are reminded of them regularly.

TIP 5

Develop a challenge culture at work

According to Vip Sandhir, CEO and founder of HighGround, creating a challenge culture is key to an organization's growth and success, as well as its employee engagement.

Getting smart people within your organization to offer feedback and challenge ideas doesn't happen overnight. As a leader, you must be willing to receive or seek advice that is essential to the success of your organization. And in today's highly competitive, fast-moving environment, businesses need everyone—and their ideas—on board. To help your organization start heading in the right direction, consider these ways to develop a challenge culture at work.

- **Foster the right environment**

When creating your company's culture, make it clear that employees are free to challenge ideas at all levels. In fact, it's expected of them. Scott Kelly, chief human resource officer of Hitachi Data Systems, says, "From day one on the job, new employees are not just encouraged, but expected to be self-starters with a solution-oriented mindset." Kelly says employees are empowered to challenge the status quo.

- **Build a culture of trust**

To ensure honest, timely, and effective feedback, all employees must trust management and each other. This starts at the top with leaders who not only talk the talk but also walk the walk. If employees see any sign of a leader's unwillingness to be challenged—or feel that their own ideas and feedback are not welcomed—they won't be willing to share them. By demonstrating that they not only seek fresh, different ideas but are also willing to act on them, leaders let everyone know it's OK to challenge management and each other. At the same time, Kelly says, "In our fast-paced world, decisions have to be made, and we can't always wait for a common consensus. In those cases, trust wins out, with employees committing to the new direction."

- **Appreciate when employees make efforts and take risks**

Organizations that are constantly looking to improve are naturally more open to being challenged by employees at all levels. But one of the easiest ways to kill a challenge culture is to incite fear around taking risks and failing. When it comes to taking risks, failure is inevitable, but being punished for doing so doesn't have to be. Eliminate this mentality from your business by giving praise and appreciation to employees who put forth their best effort and try something new—even if things didn't work out as planned. Instead of scrutinizing failure, focus on the learning experience that resulted.

- Establish and share accountability

Empowering others to challenge and offer input doesn't work unless they are held accountable. In this new model of operation, everyone must take ownership and responsibility when things go well—as well as when they don't. While employees used to be able to blame management when things went awry, that can no longer be the case under a challenge culture. To encourage this behavior, management can openly share credit for decisions that worked well and acknowledge their failures. By encouraging leaders to take responsibility, employees will be much more likely to do so too.

EI Exercise:

Schedule or informally seek one-to-one opportunities with team members. Don't only invite open feedback and challenging ideas during meetings or designated occasions. When feedback and ideas are bounced around regularly and openly, employees gain confidence to speak out and challenge ideas as they think of them.

TIP 6

Become more persuasive

"A man convinced against his will is of the same opinion still."
—Benjamin Franklin, writer, scientist, and inventor

Many people believe the way to persuade others is to win an argument or to pick out flaws in their way of thinking and their perspective. Persuasion does not work this way. While we may temporarily force or entice others to see or do things our way, they will revert to their old ways of thinking as soon as the enticement we are offering disappears. Some people believe we are born with the power of persuasion: some have it and some don't. Nothing could be further from the truth. Like all skills and competencies, you can develop persuasion through continual practice and refinement of tried-and-true skills and behaviors. You can increase your ability to be more persuasive through these means.

- **Avoid arguing or trying to force your thoughts on others**

When you argue with someone or they feel coerced, they will naturally become defensive and erect barriers. This will work counter to your persuasive efforts. Instead, allow the other person to feel that they are in control of the situation by inviting them to talk while you actively listen.

• Look for points of connection

While the other person is speaking, listen for opportunities to agree and connect. See if you can get insights into their values and the reasons they think as they do. The more shared values and connections you can make with someone, the greater the chance you can persuade them, because they will trust you and be open to your ideas. People feel more comfortable and trust others with whom they share common beliefs, values, and interests.

• Give sincere compliments

If there is something about the person you admire or that deserves praise, let them know. Everyone loves to receive a sincere compliment and receiving one from you makes them more open to anything else you have to say. Your ability to see the positive in them elevates you in their eyes and gives more credibility to everything you say and do.

• Let others think an idea is their own

The best way to be persuasive is to plant a seed in someone's mind. Instead of forcing them to do something, make suggestions. This gives them the power to make the idea their own. Take your ego out of it and allow them to take credit. An idea that we believe we came up with, or we were partly responsible for, always appeals more than one someone else is exclusively responsible for.

- Appear confident and knowledgeable

If you are not confident in your idea and your grasp of it is not solid, you won't inspire anyone else to have confidence in it. We believe those who sound confident and appear to know what they are talking about. If you are not totally convinced yourself, your lack of confidence and hesitation will show up and result in a loss of credibility and a lost opportunity to persuade others.

EI Exercise:

Enlist the help of a partner and have him or her speak on any topic, even a controversial one. Then simply repeat what you heard, noting particularly interesting points.

TIP 7

Develop signs of a highly authentic leader

"I realized I was more convincing to myself and to the people who were listening when I actually said what I thought, versus what I thought people wanted to hear me say."
—Ursula Burns, former CEO and chair of Xerox Corporation

Lately, a lot of media attention has focused on bad leaders. We hear about those who are corrupt, egotistical, and motivated solely by personal gain and self-aggrandizement. Stories of employee disengagement, bullying by management, and other reports of leadership failures appear frequently. Most great leaders, however, quietly give their best for organizations and society. These leaders make a positive difference with their staff, organizations, and society. Practice the following habits to become an authentic leader.

- **See your role as a privilege and a responsibility, not a right**

Authentic leaders see their role as one of responsibility for bringing out the best in others and doing what is best for their organization and community. They resist entitlement and seeing themselves as people ordained with special powers and privileges.

• Develop courage and self-confidence

Doing what is right, rather than what is popular, takes courage and a belief in oneself and one's abilities. Authentic leaders know their decisions will not always be popular, and they will be required at times to stand up and defend their beliefs and decisions.

• Show your true self

Genuine leaders earn trust and respect because everyone around them knows that what you see is what you get. They treat the janitor with the same respect as they do other team members and business executives. Their wives, husbands, families, and friends see the same person as do all the people they work with.

• Acknowledge your imperfections and mistakes

Genuine leaders admit their mistakes, accepting that they will never be perfect. They learn from their mistakes and move on. Those who report to genuine leaders will be more confident in pushing their own boundaries and making mistakes in the process.

• Treat others with empathy and respect

We all have preferences when dealing with others; some we like and others just seem to bring out the worst in us. Genuine leaders recognize when someone is pushing their buttons, yet they attempt to treat everyone reasonably and respectfully. They make an effort to treat everyone fairly regardless of their personal feelings toward them.

EI Exercise:

Look for ways to give back. Whether by flipping burgers at the company barbecue or coaching Little League slow pitch, avail yourself to the service of your organization and community. Find a need and share your skills and knowledge to help meet that need.

TIP 8

Do what trusted leaders do

"If you tell the truth, you don't have to remember anything."
—Mark Twain, pen name for Samuel Langhorne
Clemens, writer and entrepreneur

Perhaps nothing harms an organization more than a lack of trust in its leaders. Yet trust seems a fickle idea—difficult to develop and maintain; so easy to destroy. Trust must begin from the top to be developed throughout an organization. If people cannot trust top management, they perceive that it's "everyone for themselves." To develop a culture of trust, follow these practices.

- **Always tell the truth**

Trusted leaders tell the truth even when it is easier and more convenient to lie or leave out embarrassing facts. They also come clean and tell all, even in situations where there is little or no chance the truth will be discovered.

- **Do the right thing**

One of the easiest ways for a leader to lose trust is to do what is convenient and beneficial to himself or herself, rather than what is right. This sets up a culture where staff feel justified to primarily look out for themselves rather than doing what is most beneficial for the organization. Doing the right thing means doing the difficult thing even if at great personal risk. Leaders who do this serve as examples of integrity for others.

- **Be consistent with your message to your superiors and staff**

A sure way to develop a culture of mistrust is for managers to say one thing to those in positions above them and something different to their staff. This makes coworkers feel like they are being used, perhaps to make their manager look good. Trust, however, is developed when staff is confident that their leaders will have a consistent message regardless of the audience.

- **Share accurate information in a timely manner**

Rumors spread in the absence of accurate and timely information. Often, rumors paint a worse picture of a situation than would exist if the truth were told. Withholding information gives staff the message that they are not to be trusted to know the truth— setting up a culture of suspicion and mistrust that rumors will only feed and fuel.

- **Communicate vision and values and abide by them**

A sure way to lose trust in an organization is for management to be seen as having one set of rules for themselves and another for their staff. If there is a value statement that management has developed for the organization, they need to ensure that they follow those values themselves before expecting their staff to follow them.

EI Exercise:

Review a past difficult situation. In communicating the problem, did you present different messages to your superiors and coworkers? If you could have a do-over, how would you have made the message more consistent with both audiences? If your messaging was the same, can you point to an increased culture of trust for you personally?

TIP 9

Set up and support a
culture of creativity

*According to psychologist Robert Epstein, four core competencies
can increase the output of new and original ideas: capture your
new ideas, seek out challenging tasks, broaden your knowledge,
and surround yourself with interesting things and people.*

While all workplaces give lip service to wanting more creativity
and for their staff to come up with new and better ideas, few
take the time and effort required to set up and nurture a culture
necessary for this to happen. We may assume that creativity happens randomly and spontaneously, yet evidence points to system-
atic ways we can increase novel ideas. Here are several situations
you can employ to help nurture a creative environment.

- **Establish a system for gathering, assessing, and rewarding creativity**

Schedule ongoing, regular times to brainstorm new ideas. This
sets up the belief that creativity is an essential part of the organization. Unless staff believe leaders take creativity seriously and

reward it, they are unlikely to put the time and effort into stretching themselves.

● Hold meetings off-site

Look for interesting places to hold meetings, as far away from the workplace atmosphere as possible: a museum, historic site, college campus, or any other place that removes people from the physical things surrounding them on a daily basis.

● Give employees time to work on something of interest to them

Organizations that allow employees to spend some time on their own projects find that it helps them break out of the routine and come up with more and better ideas. Encourage staff to share with others what they are working on. In doing so, they may generate new ideas to improve their individual projects.

● Support and encourage staff toward continuous learning

Employees should be encouraged to continuously learn, whether in work-related areas or for their personal interests. Consider offering financial rewards, time off work, or recognition—formal or informal. Hold annual meetings to recognize people who made the effort to learn a new language or skill, or try out a new experience. If you can offer prizes to those who stepped the furthest outside the norm, you'll encourage others to broaden their world too.

● Put usable new ideas into practice as soon as possible

Your staff will come to believe in the value of new, original ideas when they consistently witness them being put into practice. If an idea is good and you envision strong possibilities for using it, create a plan and let everyone know the timeline to bring it to fruition. If ideas are not used, put some effort into explaining why they may be good ideas but not possible to use at this time.

EI Exercise:

At your next brainstorming meeting, invite staff to submit ideas. (Remember the rules of brainstorming: no idea is unacceptable and nobody is allowed to put down or ridicule anyone else's ideas.) After ideas are submitted, break into a couple of groups. One group defends the ideas and the other opposes them. The purpose is to have fun and overcome the fear of stepping outside the norm.

TIP 10

Develop emotionally
intelligent workplaces

*In a survey of more than 2,600 hiring managers and
human resource professionals, 71 percent stated they
valued emotional intelligence over IQ in an employee;
75 percent said they were more likely to promote a highly
emotionally intelligent worker; and 59 percent claimed
they'd pass up a candidate with a high IQ but low EI.*

Leaders are aware that emotional intelligence is important when
bringing new people on board. It is equally important, however, to develop a culture that supports and grows EI. Building an
emotionally intelligent workplace is a daunting task—far more
difficult than building your own EI. Yet you, as a leader, can create the conditions conducive to building EI in your workplace.

• Model vulnerability

An emotionally intelligent organization is one in which people are
not afraid to be vulnerable and share their fears and concerns. This
does not mean that it is OK to release any and all emotions as they

arise. Healthy work environments, however, do not require all feelings to be repressed. As in all areas, the leader must model this from the top. Leaders who appropriately share fears, sadness, and other feelings with their staff send a message that this is a safe place to work, where we don't have to be afraid of feelings leaking out.

- Cultivate self-awareness and awareness of others

You can demonstrate awareness by acknowledging difficult challenges facing your coworkers. For example, the staff in a department that is implementing new processing technology might feel stressed and overwhelmed. Leaders could share their awareness by talking about a situation in which they felt the same way while learning new technology. In meetings, leaders could take the lead in talking about their feelings in given situations and encourage their staff to do the same. This empathy helps create loyalty and dedication among teams.

- Ensure that everyone is heard and ideas can be freely expressed

Create opportunities for team sharing. Also, become aware of the different communication styles of team members. Allow time and space for quiet members of the team to be heard—set an atmosphere of respectful listening without interruption or distraction. Encourage flexibility in how team members express their ideas, such as using message boards, videos, or other forms of communication.

- Acknowledge and recognize members who exemplify your shared values

An emotionally intelligent workplace promotes an understood set of values and a shared vision. In order to work well together, teams need to be working toward a common vision. The more often goals are shared and become part of the fabric of all members, the more powerful group cohesion will become.

- **Encouraging joint activities outside the workplace**

People who spend time doing activities outside of work get to know each other as individuals and form stronger bonds that help them *at* work. This could mean going for drinks at the end of a work week, attending company retreats, going to sporting events, or spending time volunteering at a worthwhile charity. Any event where members can have fun together and get to know each other on a personal level helps groups bond, builds cohesion, and creates an atmosphere to pull together in the workplace.

EI Exercise:

In your next monthly meeting, whether in person or online, start with a few minutes of silence. This allows everyone to get focused on the meeting. Next, go around the table (or screen), asking everyone to share something going on in their lives. It works wonders in getting to know one another and increases awareness of each other's struggles, joys, and dreams. This makes for a stronger, more cooperative, and effective team.

TIP 11

Fix your broken workplace

*A Gallup Poll study found that employees who are disengaged
had 37 percent higher absenteeism, 49 percent more accidents,
and 60 percent more errors in their jobs. Over time this translated
into 18 percent lower productivity, 16 percent lower profitability,
37 percent lower job growth, and 65 percent lower share price.*

While most organizations agree, at least publicly, that developing
the right culture is important to their continued success, many
don't have a handle on creating, maintaining, and (especially) fix-
ing a culture that is broken. When things are rotten in the state of
the organization, we find it easier to blame, stick heads in the sand,
and pretend everything is going well. Apart from being unhealthy
places to work, toxic cultures also function far below the optimum
level. One sure sign of a broken culture is that employee engagement is low. Consider these ideas for rebuilding company culture.

- **Openly acknowledge the problem and honestly look for solutions**

A broken culture might result from the direct actions of management or from a hands-off management approach—one that took

little interest in the internal functioning of the organization. First, acknowledge that things are not working well. Next, leaders must authentically look for solutions instead of blaming and scapegoating. If staff believe the real purpose is to find blame, the whole thing may backfire and make the situation worse.

• Take the lead in fixing it

Whatever happened to create the broken environment, management needs to accept they had a hand in the situation and accept full responsibility for taking the lead in cleaning it up. The next step includes coming up with a plan, timeline, and process to gather feedback and ideas from staff. Be inclusive. Create a team-effort mentality that will build bridges of trust again.

• Create a safe environment

Leaders must set up an environment whereby staff feel they can speak freely without fear of repercussions. You might encourage staff to speak to someone on the leadership team they trust, or ask for a peer representative they feel safe talking with. Others might prefer to give feedback anonymously. Even more important than the opportunity to vent, staff want feedback on the solutions they offer. Developing a successful and healthy culture depends upon how much the staff feel they have been heard and listened to by their leaders.

• Roll out the results and come up with a common vision

After all the venting and discussion has taken place, leaders can summarize the results and share them. Leadership ultimately bears the responsibility to come up with a vision and forward direction for the organization. Yet staff acceptance is also crucial. When leaders implement common themes from staff feedback into the overall vision, they increase the possibility of staff buy-in. Small-group and face-to-face meetings are the best ways to share the vision of the new culture and steps for carrying it out.

- **Commit serious time and resources to the new culture**

Actions speak louder than words, and staff will want to see how serious leadership is about creating and maintaining this desired new culture. The only way to convince others that management is serious is by committing substantial time, effort, and resources—not only to developing the healthy workplace culture but also to ensuring it carries on after the initial enthusiasm has died down. Commit to regular timelines in the future for review and evaluation, and to ensuring that staff have the necessary time and resources to continue this valuable work. Your staff's commitment to a healthy work culture will only be as great as they believe their organization's leadership's commitment to be.

EI Exercise:

If you find yourself in a toxic workplace, share your feelings in an honest and vulnerable way. Some leaders may see sharing honest feelings as a sign of weakness; however, the opposite is true. Most staff will feel relieved and appreciate leaders who have the courage to share their human side with them. It will give staff official approval to open up, be honest, and share their own feelings—a crucial step to moving beyond toxicity.

TIP 12

Develop future leaders

*The leader of tomorrow will have to be adaptable,
flexible, willing, and able to master new skills
more quickly than his or her predecessors.*

The challenges of tomorrow's workplace include rapid technological advancement along with changing expectations from millennials and Gen Zers. Job security and lifelong guarantees of work are relics from another era. Any routine workplace roles risk being replaced by artificial intelligence and bots that can make decisions much more quickly and with a higher degree of accuracy. As organizations increasingly flatten in structure, leaders expect more decision-making at all levels. In this new environment, the following action points will be critical for your future.

- **Effectively communicate a vision that inspires others**

Tomorrow's leaders will motivate others in the organization through their ability to share a compelling vision. The workforce of tomorrow wants more than pay and benefits; they expect to contribute toward a worthwhile goal. Rabbi Stephen Baars, author of *Win: Change Your Thinking, Change Your Destiny*, states, "When we plan right and establish real, motivating, and gut grabbing goals, then we become innately and unbelievably motivated."

● Lead from the heart

Future leaders who are emotionally aware of themselves and able to manage their emotions effectively will be more likely to gain loyalty and buy-in from their staff, suppliers, and clients. According to Kerry Wekelo, author of *Culture Infusion*, "Leading from the heart is looking at each situation through compassion and kindness and having empathy for each team member. When you lead from your heart, you will get to know your team (whether they report to you or not) and their unique skills and insights."

● Be a quick and lifelong learner at a macro level

Leaders of tomorrow will be unable to keep up with the intimate details of all the changes happening both inside and outside their organizations. So they will have to find content experts—people they can rely on to keep them informed. In this way, they will stay current with the latest technological and environmental changes. Tomorrow's leaders will spend a great deal of time educating themselves on changes that are affecting their organization today and into the future.

● Understand future demographics

The ability to communicate effectively and with wider, diverse audiences will become increasingly important for leaders.

- **Adapt**

The rapid pace of technological change combined with changing tastes, desires, and marketing techniques will require tomorrow's leader to rapidly change direction—constantly adjusting to a new reality. Instead of dreading chaos and uncertainty, they will learn to accept those conditions as the new norm.

- **Develop trust and earn respect**

Amid such rapid change, organizations need trusted leaders if they are to thrive. Leaders must build that trust by being authentic, open, and transparent. This means that a leader's words must be consistent with, and backed up by, his or her actions. They must treat all members of the organization fairly and equitably, leaving no room for favoritism or nepotism. Otherwise, highly skilled and valuable staff will look for work in organizations where they will be accorded respect and recognition for their skills and efforts.

- **Put people and the organization first**

Leaders of tomorrow will constantly be looking for ways to grow and advance the people in the organization. Apart from seeing that their organization is thriving financially, they will see developing coworkers as a primary goal. Future leaders will look for ways to show appreciation to their people and find ways to make them feel genuinely valued.

El Exercise:

Identify potential leaders in your organization and share magazine articles, websites, or videos on developing emotional intelligence. Or give them a copy of this book.

TIP 13

Recognize awesome employees

"When people are financially invested, they want a return. When people are emotionally invested, they want to contribute." —Simon Sinek, author of Start with Why

Most employers when asked what they look for in a potential new hire will bring up attitude. Many will rate attitude as important, often more so than ability, skill, and technical knowledge. While the actual skills needed to perform a job can usually be taught, soft skills and attitude are more nebulous and difficult to change. Employers today are increasingly on the lookout for candidates with the right attitude and people skills, whom they can train for the other skills. Notice which employees display these traits.

● Show respect and consideration for others

People who are aware of themselves are also more attuned to the emotions of those around them. Because of this, they develop strong, positive working relationships with their coworkers. This builds camaraderie and loyalty and increases the capacity and efficiency of the organization.

• Willingness to speak up

Excellent employees speak up when they recognize a need, especially if others are avoiding or overlooking an important issue. Knowing when and how to bring up an issue allows them to broach sensitive topics that scare others away. They sense when an issue can be addressed publicly and when it is best left to private conversation. Their skills at asking questions with sensitivity allow them to ask without offending and putting others on the defensive.

• Focus on what is important

Valued employees focus on the job at hand without being distracted by bright shiny objects or minor disturbances. They discern what is important and in what order, and have the ability to prioritize. Although focused, they also possess strong people skills that keep them from being rude or insensitive to colleagues who disrupt them while working on an important and timely task.

• Display confidence but not egotism

Great employees are confident in their abilities but hold their egos in check. They display patience with others who need their help. They don't put down team members—even those who may possess less talent and ability. This approachable side of their personality makes others feel comfortable coming to them with issues and concerns they might not otherwise bring up.

- **Never say, "It's not my responsibility"**

Exceptional employees will not walk past a problem or something they could help with because it is not in their job description. They see their role as helping in any manner they are able and are always willing to give of their time and knowledge. They view their role as larger than their job description and look for ways to contribute to the organization.

- **Know when to have fun and when to be serious**

Great employees help lighten up the workplace with their sense of humor, when appropriate, but also know when it is time to be serious and get down to business. When a coworker is feeling down or struggling, they are the first to offer a listening ear, words of encouragement, or condolences.

- **Always look for ways to improve**

The most valued employees will be the first to come up with suggestions and ideas on how to improve their work environment and will take initiative to make it happen. Change to them is seen as a positive, an opportunity to improve. The exceptional employee who embraces change is a great ally to management, helping overcome the resistance of others to change.

EI Exercise:

Start a "you're awesome" gift card program. When an employee exhibits some of the above criteria, email him or her a digital gift card to a coffee shop or local eatery. If possible, open up the program so all employees can gift a card to especially helpful team members.

TIP 14

Enjoy the benefits of being vulnerable

"You have to be honest and authentic and not hide. I think the leader today has to demonstrate both transparency and vulnerability, and with that comes truthfulness and humility."
—Howard Schultz, former Starbucks CEO and chair

As noted earlier, being vulnerable and showing yourself to others is actually a sign of courage and self-confidence. Successful leaders know when the time and place is right to show their real and authentic selves. As a vulnerable leader, you reap these great benefits.

• **Experience decreased tension and stress at work**

Have you ever worked somewhere with an elephant in the room? Everyone's blood pressure rises, trying to figure out ways to avoid the uncomfortable topic. This stress could be decreased considerably by acknowledging such topics and allowing people to talk about them. If everyone sees that their leaders don't tiptoe around discomfort but bring up the issue for discussion, they will feel freer to talk about it as well.

- **Appreciate an increased flow of ideas, creativity, and innovation**

By admitting their mistakes, managers give their staff more room to contribute their feedback and ideas. Leaders who acknowledge when they make poor decisions, and are still able forgive themselves, model to those under them that it is OK to take risks and try something new. This leads to more ideas coming from all levels, creating a more dynamic, competitive organization.

- **Identify problems earlier**

Many times people are afraid to bring bad news and problems to their leaders. By the time the leaders find out what is really going on, a great deal of damage could have been done. Staff who witness their leaders being vulnerable and admitting their mistakes are more likely to come forward without fear of retribution.

- **Create a fun workplace**

A leader who is open, vulnerable, and authentic raises the mood of the work environment and creates a healthy, vibrant atmosphere that everyone looks forward to being part of.

- **Watch how emotional connections lead to less turnover**

A great deal of research points out that being emotionally connected to a workplace often serves as a deciding factor on whether or not people will stay. With open, honest, and authentic leadership, staff at all levels are more likely to feel an emotional connection and believe that those leaders have their best interests at heart. Consequently, they are less likely to jump ship, even for more money or benefits.

EI Exercise:

Name three mistakes you've made in the workplace that you don't want to talk about. Pick one and figure out how to talk about it in a near-future staff meeting.

TIP 15

Give your team a performance boost

*"Coming together is a beginning; keeping together
is progress; working together is success."*
—Henry Ford, founder of Ford Motor Company

Much has been written about the importance of teamwork in reaching objectives. Yet less thought and effort has gone into creating and developing effective teams. Groups of people are often thrown together for major projects without much effort—neglecting to develop them into a motivated team that will work well together toward a common goal. While most organizations do well with the technical aspects of team projects, such as timelines and action plans, they fall short on the people-building part. With a little effort, thought, and foresight, many of the problems that plague teams can be avoided. As a team leader, here are a number of things you should consider when putting a team together.

- **Make sure everyone understands and buys into the "why"**

People generally will put minimum effort into something they consider unimportant or see as a make-work project. At the beginning, make sure everyone understands the importance of the task and how it fits into the organization's goals. Take time to answer questions. Explain why there needs to be a team instead of everyone working individually. It is crucial that every member buy into the concept that a *team* can accomplish more than an *individual.*

- Model the behavior you wish to see from your team

Modeling behavior includes sharing any frustrations in the course of a project and readily admitting mistakes—taking full responsibility. This builds trust and helps meld the team into a working unit.

- Keep communication direct and within the team as much as possible

While your superiors may require updates on your team and its work, only share progress reports—keep the dynamics (what is happening within the team) out of it. Team members will lose trust if they feel you are sharing everything. If you witness issues with any members that are affecting their performance, take them aside for a conversation. Prepare for these conversations ahead of time so you don't come across as angry or accusatory. Point out what you have noticed. For example, "I thought you sounded angry when Ryan questioned your knowledge of outsourcing. Tell me more about that." Ask open-ended questions that start with "It sounded to me like . . ." or, "It felt to me like. . . ." Only bring up the behavior you observed; never make judgments about why someone may have behaved as they did. It is possible that what you observed was not what the team member intended. For example, never ask, "Were you angry because you thought Ryan was getting more attention than you?"

- **Schedule a short check-in at the beginning of every meeting**

Limit the time for this short emotional check-in. Be clear that this is not a personal therapy session but a way to get grounded before settling into the work. Perhaps a team member isn't feeling well, is experiencing a serious personal problem, or is struggling because a family member has passed away. In this brief sharing period, other members can understand why someone in the group might not be their usual self. This also helps the group leader see if someone needs attention and time outside of the group.

- **Celebrate wins and acknowledge individual contributions**

Celebrate successful steps along the way. For example, finishing a report that was well-received could call for buying lattes for everyone. Recognize everyone's unique contribution and how it fits into the overall success of the team. Various personalities bring different aspects to the group and contribute in different ways: the stickler for details ensures that valuable information isn't overlooked, and the jokester lightens the mood, lessening the stress and enhancing the team process.

- **Get out of the office on occasion**

The best way to get to know people you work with is to spend time together away from the office. We can often learn more about a colleague from a short amount of time over a drink or fun activity away from work than from years in the workplace. Seeing others in a relaxed atmosphere gives us a greater perspective on their unique challenges and abilities.

El Exercise:

At the beginning of your next project, make the WIIFMs ("What's in it for me?") clear. Remind members how working on the project benefits them personally: increased visibility to leadership, chance of promotion, potential award, skill acquisition to increase future job opportunities, etc. Be specific—use examples from past team successes.

Develop mental toughness

"The only way of finding the limits of the possible is by going beyond them into the impossible." —Arthur C. Clarke, science fiction author and cowriter of 2001, A Space Odyssey

If we look at the achievements of everyone who has made a difference in the world—from Thomas Edison to Mother Teresa—we will find at least one trait they shared: a high degree of mental toughness. They kept moving toward their goals, enduring ridicule from many naysayers and doubters. Mental toughness is not something we are born with, as many believe. It is a set of characteristics we can *all* attain. Here are some habits you should develop.

- **Manage your emotions**

Mentally tough people have learned when, and with whom, they can safely share their feelings: people they can trust and count on to be supportive. They have developed the ability to control their emotions and impulses in situations where this would be seen as a sign of weakness and could be used against them.

- **Push your boundaries for increased self-confidence**

To attempt something outside the scope of your "norm" requires a high degree of self-confidence. Mentally tough people are not born with more self-confidence; they acquire this by continually pushing their boundaries and moving beyond their fears. This expands their capacity to take risks and deal with the setbacks and failures so inevitable before a major breakthrough. The knowledge that they will eventually achieve a breakthrough further increases their stamina, resilience, and mental toughness.

- **Choose those you associate with wisely**

Mentally tough people hang out with other positive-thinking individuals with whom they share common goals and aspirations. They support one another and celebrate each other's achievements. Negative people drain energy. When you're around negative people, tune out the negativity and limit your interaction. In this way, you can abstain from negative people taking up your valuable time, energy, and focus.

- **Face your fears**

When faced with a calculated, necessary risk to reach their objectives, mentally tough people find ways to overcome their fears and go for it. They know that any worthwhile achievement involves the possibility of failure. Considering the worst-case scenario, they decide they can withstand it and keep going, never letting fear stop them. For them, failure is not the worst of possibilities; the worst-case scenario is having regrets at the end of their lives about things they didn't attempt.

- Maintain boundaries and say no when necessary

Many people say yes when they don't want to do something, just to please others. They often regret this afterward and complain that they should have said no. Mentally tough people learn to say no without hedging their answer or making excuses for why they are unable or unwilling to do something. This demonstrates that they are not pushovers and should not be approached with unreasonable demands on their time and energy.

- Don't compare yourself to others

Those who have developed mental toughness do not pay much attention to what others think of them or compare themselves to others. They have well-defined goals in life that motivate and drive them. While they are open to the opinions of others they respect, they ultimately take responsibility for their decisions and outcomes and do not blame others or circumstances for their failures. They continually strive to do better than they did the day before.

EI Exercise:

Mentally tough people possess great self-discipline and adhere to a strict regime regarding their own health and wellness habits. They seldom take the easy way out by not adhering to their exercise, eating, and sleeping patterns. Put in writing your plan for keeping physically fit and healthy. Include ways to achieve the adequate rest necessary for your overall well-being. Doggedly stay true to your plan.

TIP 17

Be a leader who attracts loyal people

Is loyalty dead?

Loyalty in the workplace has been spiralling downward for decades. Today, people in their twenties change jobs an average of every two years. The old contract of loyalty—whereby the employee stayed with the organization in exchange for lifetime security—has been gone for some time now. Yet some organizations still inspire high levels of loyalty. While a number of factors come into play in the loyalty equation, leadership is still a major one. Consider how your leadership attributes inspire loyalty.

- **Be fair and consistent**

Nobody likes to work for a phony. Younger generations are increasingly unwilling to accept direction from people for whom they have little respect. Good leaders can be counted on to say what they mean and do what they say. Their interactions with staff, those above them, and their customers and partners remain fair and consistent.

- **Serve those you lead**

Loyalty-inspiring leaders sincerely see their part as role-modeling for, motivating, and improving those they lead. They regard their staff as more than a means to their own promotion up the ladder. Instead, they find meaning and purpose in advancing and bringing out the best in those they lead. Success to them is counted in the number of people they have helped advance in the organization. In private conversations regarding their work, they love to include stories about those employees and their accomplishments.

- **Encourage and support staff in their development**

The best leaders continually look for ways to encourage staff members to develop themselves, not only in the workplace but also in their personal lives. They look for opportunities to challenge those under them and use their resources to provide training and opportunities to advance in the organization. When such opportunities are not available internally, inspiring managers will even look for opportunities externally. Inspiring leaders are more afraid of their staff members stagnating than they are of losing them.

- **Trust your staff**

With the confidence of their leader, staff are more apt to take on challenges and risk failure. People who know that their leaders have their backs are more apt to take risks than those who fear the consequences of making mistakes.

- **Share your vision**

Leaders make it clear to their staff what it takes to be successful in the organization and share where they see the organization going.

Their positive energy and belief in those they are working with is contagious and boosts the energy of those around them.

- Jump in and help

Regardless of what positions they hold, inspiring leaders work alongside those they lead every chance they get. They never see the work their staff does as being too far beneath them to participate in. If emergencies strike, inspiring leaders are the first on the scene, offering to do whatever is necessary to get the job done. They demonstrate that they don't expect anyone to do a task they themselves are unwilling to do.

El Exercise:

Talk to any inspiring leader, and that individual will be able to share an amazing wealth of information about his or her team—not only work history but details about families, hobbies, and outside interests. Take time to check in with your team members; be willing to slow down and talk with employees in the hallway, at their desks, or during one-to-one Zoom calls. Additionally, plan to meet with your team outside of the office for a fun get-together. Include remote workers by sending a gift basket or another theme-related memento.

TIP 18

Earn respect

"The challenge of leadership is to be strong, but not rude; be kind, but not weak; be bold, but not bully; be thoughtful, but not lazy; be humble, but not timid; be proud, but not arrogant; have humor, but without folly." —Jim Rohn, entrepreneur and author

While someone may have advanced in their organization to a level of leadership, that alone will not earn them respect. Their title and position may earn them extra pay and benefits, but respect is something that does not automatically come with the position. It has to be earned—one of the most difficult things for a leader to acquire. Respected leaders are not always liked by everyone, nor always popular. A leader may be well-liked as a person yet be a weak leader who is afraid to make difficult decisions. On the other hand, some leaders intimidate their subordinates and use fear as a way of getting things done. None of these leaders will earn the respect of their followers. If we take a closer look at leaders who have walked the difficult paths that have earned them respect, we will see the following traits—traits for you to emulate.

- **Be willing to do what you expect others to do**

Lead by example. Your efforts will set a standard for the rest of the organization. If you are unwilling to put the extra time and effort into a project that you expect from your staff, you will be seen as a hypocrite. Leaders who are highly respected put in at least as much time and effort as those they serve.

- **Believe that people strive to do their best**

When preparing to give negative feedback, look for opportunities to turn it into a learning and growth opportunity for the employee rather than a form of punishment. This is your chance to bring out the best in a staff member. Respected leaders believe in and trust those they are in charge of until proven wrong.

- **Give credit where it's due and do what's right instead of what's popular**

Well-respected leaders are confident and well-grounded, secure in who they are and in their abilities. As a result, they don't run away from tough decisions even though their decision may not be popular. When things are going well, they look for ways to give credit to their staff. Even when a leader's own idea is successful, he or she will try to deflect credit and shine it on those who implemented it. When a tough decision needs to be made, strong leaders make it quickly and avoid blaming others.

- **Take responsibility when things don't go as expected**

While it may be easier to weasel out of taking responsibility, respected leaders always take the high road. They take responsibility even when mistakes were made by someone reporting to them, even though it would be easy to shift the responsibility.

"The buck stops here" is a motto they live by. These leaders have their people's backs and are willing to defend them to those above them when necessary.

- **Don't show favoritism**

Insecure leaders want people around them who will not threaten or challenge them, so they promote yes people. On the other hand, respected leaders invite challenge and pushback, knowing they will become better leaders and people. They are in constant learning and growing mode and are supportive of staff members who show initiative. While it is tempting to favor people who stroke our egos, respected leaders rise above that and make a sincere attempt to reward talent and hard work regardless of their personal feelings about the person.

- **Encourage others to take risks**

Respected leaders encourage those they are leading to take risks. They stand behind them when things don't work out as planned. They believe that openness and honesty are the best ways to operate—encouraging others to come to them when things have gone wrong instead of trying to hide the problem.

EI Exercise:

Consider that challenging, high-risk/high-reward project you've had in the back of your mind. Assume you have the go-ahead and put together your dream team. Think of your planning as a way of further enhancing a respected reputation. Include risk-takers, detail-minded staff, and that person who wants a second chance to prove himself or herself.

Plan carefully when you have to fire an employee

Ask any manager what the least favorite part of their job is, and chances are they will tell you it's having to fire someone.

It is a gut-wrenching job. Perhaps the person being fired has been slacking, has a serious attitude problem, and dissed their coworkers and management. On the other hand, this person could simply be doing his or her best—a decent person who just lacks the ability to perform the job to a necessary standard. Regardless, firing should be a final option, used only after repeated, sincere attempts to bring the person up to the necessary level have been exhausted. While firing will never be a pleasant experience, you can minimize the discomfort and pain that will be felt by the terminated person.

- **Pick the right time and place**

Don't even think of terminating an employee in any other way than a face-to-face meeting. The person deserves at least this much. The other staff in the organization, who will find out, will lose respect for a manager who does not have the courage or consideration to fire face-to-face. Think through the time and place of your meeting. A good time is when other staff are away or have gone home. Emotions will run high, and the individual may experience various degrees of shock, anger, shame, or humiliation. This is not the time and place for them to be talking to colleagues.

- **Prepare yourself emotionally**

Check your emotions before going into the meeting. You will also experience strong emotions. When you start feeling the urge to give in to those emotions, give yourself time and wait them out. Silently count to ten, think of something else, but wait until you are calm before speaking. Another technique to try while in the meeting is to push your feet firmly into the floor. This will help keep you centered.

- **Avoid blame or finger-pointing**

While the individual may have been totally responsible for what brought on the firing, rehashing everything will only make things worse. Simply state that things didn't work out. Acknowledge that you've talked about the issue and potential consequences before, and this is the consequence. If you are truly sorry, say so. If not, don't. Allow the person's dignity to remain as intact as possible without being inauthentic or insincere.

- **Be both firm and fair**

Summarize the main points of what lead to your decision and leave it there. Be firm and don't open up new areas for discussion. Expect various emotions ranging from shock, denial, and anger, to grief; you may encounter variations and combinations of each.

If the person is in shock and denial, simply repeat the message. Don't get into a debate or defend your decision. If encountering anger or grief, acknowledge but don't get into further discussions. If grief, keep moving forward and focus on the future.

- **Clear up all the details with sensitivity**

Be prepared with all the details necessary upon termination, such as severance pay, unused vacation time, returning company property, end dates of benefits, etc. Allow the person to clean up their belongings without coworkers around. If this is not possible in the moment, set up a time as soon as possible to do this.

EI Exercise:

Planning is crucial. While there are many times when spontaneity is the best course of action, this is not one of them. The more prepared you are, the less chance of things going off the rails. Check over your script with someone and rehearse it, preferably with someone in HR, and practice until you are familiar with it.

TIP 20

Be willing to learn

Leaders high in emotional intelligence are constant learners—always asking themselves questions in efforts to continually improve.

Many studies have shown a direct, negative impact of bad leaders on employee morale, retention, and productivity. In contrast, workplaces with high levels of emotionally intelligent leadership stand out for their high employee retention rates as well as their reputation as great places to work. Here are five questions you should ask yourself all the time.

- **Did I empower my team enough?**

Leaders constantly walk a fine line between giving their team enough freedom and taking charge when necessary to prevent things from going off the rails. Effective leaders allow their team maximum freedom by allowing them to create, take calculated risks, and learn from mistakes. These leaders are constantly asking themselves where they are in terms of giving their people freedom versus stepping in when they see things going in the wrong direction.

- **Am I listening and understanding well enough?**

Great leaders are great communicators. As well as being able to get their messages and ideas across, they recognize the importance of being effective listeners. They excel not only at giving clear messages, but also at being aware of what is going on with their people. This helps them understand their teams and gives them early indicators of what their concerns and challenges are. They become aware of issues and deal with them before they become crises.

- **Did I recognize my people when they went over and above?**

Look for opportunities to show appreciation to team members who are doing something well. Blanket appreciation is the lazy way out and can actually be a demotivator for those who are going above and beyond. Because of this awareness, effective leaders spend the time and effort to get to know the roles of their staff in order to spot those who are performing above what is expected of them.

- **Am I supporting my people in achieving their goals?**

Emotionally intelligent leaders not only know the roles of the people who work in their area, but they are also aware of their individual career desires and goals. They want to know if their staff members' current roles are satisfying their overall work goals and if they are learning and growing toward those goals. These leaders care about the benefits someone brings to the organization and also want to support their overall career—and they let their people know it.

- **Am I making my vision for the organization clear and consistent?**

One of the chief roles of a leader is sharing a clear and consistent vision for their organization with their staff. They desire that everyone be aware of the goals and mission *and* how their individual roles contribute to that outcome. An emotionally intelligent leader is open, transparent, and timely in sharing changes within the organization, alongside the original goals and vision. Being kept in the loop of organizational information increases employee trust and loyalty.

EI Exercise:

The above five questions make for a solid starting point in building emotional intelligence. Based on your past experience—perhaps a mistake you have made—come up with your own personalized question six.

TIP 21

Work to be a sought-after humble leader

"Leaders who champion others wind up with teams who exhibit lower absenteeism, lower attrition and increased team confidence, as well as higher team performance."
—*Dan Pontefract, author of* Lead. Care. Win.

For some of the world's great leaders, the trait of humility doesn't necessarily make the list. Bigger-than-life leaders such as Steve Jobs, Elon Musk, or Bill Gates would likely be described as visionary, bold, and charismatic. Yet, if we look more closely, we find leaders who are known to be humble and laid back.

A survey of computer product firms published in the *Journal of Management* found that humble leaders resulted in higher performing teams, better collaboration, and flexibility. The authoritarian leadership style is out. In vogue is the servant-leader: humble, collaborative, and driven by the well-being of his or her staff and the organization. Since millennials and Gen Zers are not afraid to leave jobs when they are not feeling fulfilled and appreciated, organizations are paying more attention to the type of leadership they thrive in. You can follow the example of humble leaders by adopting these practices.

• Do not abuse authority

We have all heard horror stories of power hungry, status-seeking leaders and the damage they do to those under them and ultimately to the organization. Humble leaders see themselves more as coaches and mentors, always looking for ways to encourage and bring out the best in others. Instead of keeping authority and control, they look for ways to delegate and give others the opportunity to expand their leadership potential.

• Constantly look to promote others

Humble leaders understand the need for others to succeed. They promote based on skill, talent, and hard work. Unlike self-serving leaders, they are not likely to be impressed by those who simply ingratiate themselves. Their humility allows them to focus on the big picture, understanding that the overall success of the organization will be improved by developing authentic, deserving leaders.

• Model and support collaboration

Rather than fostering competition, humble leaders encourage and reward collaboration. This increases teamwork capabilities and results in increased trust among team members. On the other hand, heightened competition between team members results in mistrust with time and energy spent on vying for position rather than focusing on the work of the team. When collaboration becomes the norm, team members feel more relaxed and able to bring their full abilities and skills to the workplace.

- **Model integrity and trust**

Humble leaders do not build up their reputations with shows of aggrandizement and pretense. With them, what you see is what you get. Instead of flashy words and talk, they back up what they say with action. Team- and community-oriented, they look for ways to be helpful and to learn more about the organization. They might be found pitching in to help in any situation that requires immediate attention. This kind of engagement earns them respect and trust from those who work under them.

- **Support your staff**

Humble leaders look for opportunities to catch their staff doing something. They focus on solutions and learning opportunities, rather than on meting out blame and punishment. Being humble, however, does not mean they are pushovers. They set firm boundaries and are clear about what they look for in others. Those who work for a humble leader will know what is expected of them and don't have to be worried about being criticized, called out in public, or humiliated in front of their coworkers. They know that even if they have made a mistake, they will be listened to, understood, and given the opportunity to make changes.

- **Admit mistakes and shortcomings**

Humble leaders do not need to feel like the smartest person in the room. They are secure enough in themselves that they do not feel threatened when others know more than they do. When they make mistakes, they openly admit to them. If someone comes up with a better idea, they don't feel it is beneath them to accept it. According to Dan Pontefract, author of *Lead. Care. Win,*

"Admitting to a mistake and then saying sorry demonstrates a willingness to make a wrong known swiftly, and to take accountability for it. Those two acts not only portray vulnerability but a wonderful example of honest leadership."

- Be the first to take responsibility and the last to take credit

Humble leaders take responsibility when things don't work out. On the other hand, they will graciously give credit to others when things go well. They have a team-first mindset and are always looking for ways to support and get the most from their teams. When their teams do well, they seldom take credit themselves, realizing that praise, appreciation, and acknowledgment motivate people to give their best.

EI Exercise:

Pick one trait mentioned above that you would like to improve upon. Practice and take note of how many times you demonstrate the trait next week.

TIP 22

Retain remote workers

A 2019 survey found that 82 percent of staff would think about leaving their organization for a more empathetic one. Seventy-eight percent stated they would work longer hours if they knew their employer cared about them.

Since the onset of COVID-19, our workplaces have seen massive disruption, forcing an unprecedented number of employees to work from home. Some welcomed this change; others found it difficult both mentally and emotionally. And many continued to foster remote teams even after the pandemic waned.

One of the biggest challenges faced by remote employees is remaining engaged with their organizations and feeling that their employer understands what they are going through. As face-to-face interactions decrease, the need for connection has grown, so employers must work to assure their staff that they are thought of and cared for. Here are five tips for emotionally intelligent leaders who want to retain their remote employees.

- **Do not assume everything is OK if you don't get feedback**

With a remote team, leaders find it more difficult to spot some-one who is struggling mentally and emotionally. Outward signs of stress—often revealed in body language and general appearance—can easily be hidden. Employees who are struggling may be hesi-tant to reach out to their supervisors or others for fear of appearing needy, dependent, or unable to do their work.

- **Screen time is the second-best option**

While screen time does not take the place of in-person interac-tion, it beats email and phone communication. At least we can see the other person's face, which gives us some feeling of being connected. Leaders can demonstrate that they care by limiting email to information-sharing and using screen time for any kind of in-depth discussions.

- **Increase personal contact**

Leaders need to spend more time checking in on their employees regularly, preferably via Zoom or another screen platform. This is *not* an excuse to monitor or micromanage their work but to genuinely make connection.

- **Look for opportunities to set up supportive networks**

Not all people who work remotely have the same struggles. Some look after children who may be home from school. Others may be caregivers who look after elderly parents. Talk with HR about how you might set up networking meetings for staff—to connect with others who experience similar issues. Employee assistance programs could also take the lead in setting up and facilitating such groups.

- Celebrate successes and special events

Although your team might not share the same space, you can work to build connections. Gather via Zoom each month to recognize employee "wins." Or create virtual events just for fun, such as "Wear Your Ugliest Sweater," where you offer prizes to the winners with the most votes. Provide articles of clothing with the company logo to be worn during meetings, creating a feeling of group-belonging. Also, ask your team for *their* ideas.

EI Exercise:

Compile a list of local, trusted external organizations that provide support for various problems remote staff may face—or obtain such a list from human resources. Share the list with your staff and employees, encouraging them to make use of services provided.

TIP 23

Prepare for times of crisis

"Your initial response is by far the most important . . . All the things that are being done now should have been done a lot earlier." —Oscar Muñoz, former president of rail operator CSX and former CEO of United Airlines, as reported to CNBC regarding the Norfolk Southern train derailment in East Palestine, Ohio.

When a crisis happens, we humans tend to exhibit a fight-or-flight response. The unexpected launches us into a place of fear. We look to our leaders more than ever to provide us with guidance, hope, and support. While our leaders will not have all the answers, we expect them to help locate those who do, provide moral support and direction, and shine a light so we can find our way to a better place. We are looking for someone to trust, someone who will have our best interests at heart. This requires leaders who manage their emotions and help us manage ours. Display your emotional intelligence by taking these steps in times of crisis.

- **Develop empathy**

In difficult times, leaders are judged not necessarily by what they said or did, but by how they made people feel. They may say the right words, as if reading from a teleprompter, yet many people will sense if those leaders are simply saying what is expected. Leaders who are genuinely empathetic and concerned for the needs of those they represent will come across as honest, sincere, and authentic.

- **Increase self-awareness**

Like all of us, leaders experience the full range of emotions. Because of their power to influence, they need to keep those emotions in check even more than the rest of us do. During times of crisis, the most effective leaders control their fear and their impulse to avoid responsibility. To do so, they must be aware of what they are feeling and what emotions may be most difficult for them to manage, and then work to bring them under control before communicating publicly.

- **Foster adaptability**

During a crisis, the situation may change drastically and constantly without warning. Leaders must move along with the crisis *as* it changes. Highly adaptable leaders don't worry about not having all the answers, about being vulnerable, or about relying on others who are more knowledgeable. They provide assurances and comfort in letting us know that answers will be found.

- **Nurture social awareness**

Emotionally intelligent leaders are aware of how a crisis affects those involved. Before communicating publicly, the aware leader will show sensitivity for those directly impacted by the crisis, as well as the community as a whole. Such leaders prepare in advance to speak and understand the social context, so they can avoid making tone deaf statements.

- Work toward strong, authentic communication

In addition to good communications skills, leaders must also speak in a natural-sounding style with authenticity. People who are used to hearing them speak will pick up when they communicate differently than usual, and listeners will question their genuineness and authenticity. Communicating through a crisis is often the most difficult thing leaders have to do, pushed far out of their comfort zones. The best leaders rise to the occasion and allow the best of themselves to come through.

EI Exercise:

Develop or update your company's crisis plans, working with human resources, public relations, and outside consultants if necessary. Game out as many scenarios as you can foresee, including active shooter events.

TIP 24

Develop empathy, the most important leadership skill

"When you listen with empathy to another person, you give that person psychological air." —Stephen Covey, educator and author

In a recent study carried out by Development Dimensions International (DDI), empathy was discovered to be the biggest single leadership skill needed today. According to Richard S. Wellins, senior vice president of DDI, "Being able to listen and respond with empathy is overwhelmingly the one interaction skill that outshines all other skills."

Companies are responding to this reality by sending their leaders to empathy training. According to the *Wall Street Journal,* 20 percent of employers now offer empathy training, which is up substantially from ten years prior. Here are compelling reasons that empathy is the most important leadership skill you should develop.

• **Empathy leads to less absenteeism and greater job satisfaction**

Staff who feel witnessed, heard, and appreciated feel more satisfied with their work and as a result miss fewer days on the job.

If employees feel that nobody cares, why should they? Increased absenteeism decreases morale because coworkers who have to pick up the slack become resentful. This can create a downward spiral in terms of employee morale and absenteeism rates.

- **Engagement increases when staff feel appreciated**

When someone close to you notices how you are feeling, or tells you how much they appreciate something you have done for them, do you automatically feel the urge to do more for them? Similarly, when leadership demonstrates to employees that they care, the reciprocity reaction kicks in: employees want to put in more effort. Still, many organizations miss this basic yet very important point when it comes to leadership behaviors. Leaders of successful organizations continually look for ways to notice, compliment, and show their appreciation to their staff.

- **Empathy leads to people working together more effectively in teams**

When employees feel valued and appreciated, not only do they want to do more in their work, but they also want to do more for their fellow employees. When empathy is demonstrated at the top, it spreads throughout the organization, resulting in an increase in teamwork, a decrease in staff conflict, and a decrease in workplace disruption.

- **People who believe their leaders care about them stay longer in an organization**

Every organization struggles to retain talented staff. One of the most common reasons cited by people leaving an organization is lack of trust in and appreciation from those they report to. Empathy increases feelings of trust, and staff will feel valued and cared about. We are more likely to stay—both in an organization and in personal relationships—when we feel like we are heard, appreciated, and cared about.

● Empathy within organizations leads to an increase in creativity and new ideas

People who feel heard and appreciated perceive that they are an integral part of an organization. As a result, they tend to risk more and look for ways to add value to the organization. They are more likely to invest time and energy coming up with new ideas, processes, and methods to improve their own work and move the organization forward. They feel that their success and that of the organization are interrelated, boosting their desire to find new, better, and more efficient ways of working.

EI Exercise:

DDI, as quoted in the *Wall Street Journal*, suggests practicing these traits: Use phrases like "I hear that you're feeling angry," to recognize a person's emotions without being judgmental. Be authentic and sincere even when you disagree with someone's feelings. Use phrases that both acknowledge emotions and still hold employees accountable.

TIP 25

Learn how to deliver bad news

While it is impossible to predict and manage the repercussions from unwelcome news, emotionally intelligent leaders know how to minimize the damage.

Delivering bad news is never an easy task, but there are ways for you to carry out this unpleasant task that are more effective than others. Consider your delivery itself. Fallout from bad news can't be avoided; yet in many cases, the fallout stems more from how the news was announced, rather than the news itself. Handled well, the organization can adapt, move forward, and keep its reputation intact. When handled clumsily, with little thought and regard for those who are affected, it can leave a long-lasting stain on an organization. Consider the following steps when delivering bad news.

- **Appreciate that timing is crucial**

Deliver unwanted information at the right time, not prematurely or unduly late. Delivering it before you know enough details will cause fear and anxiety; delaying until after all the facts are known can cause suspicion. Do your best to get in front of bad news—delays can cause rumors that magnify the situation in a negative way. Emotionally intelligent leaders will also consider the timing that works best for their staff.

- **Stick to the facts**

The less that can be said, the better. Do not sugarcoat or minimize the situation, but do not make the situation sound worse than it is. Present facts clearly and succinctly. Leaders need to be prepared with exactly what they are going to say and avoid going off script.

- **Be open and nondefensive**

Leaders high in emotional intelligence are prepared for anger, accusations, and pushback when delivering bad news. They know that becoming defensive will only exacerbate the situation. Staying nondefensive as people express normal emotions will allow opportunity for real dialogue. Emotionally aware leaders can also share their own feelings but need to avoid finger-pointing.

- **Look for something positive**

If possible, find something about the situation that is positive. Perhaps it could be a lesson learned that will help in the future. Sometimes situations that look bleak in the moment turn out to have unanticipated positive outcomes.

- **Treat everyone fairly and respectfully**

Everyone will be watching to see how leaders handle the situation and how all affected parties are treated. Almost all organizations claim that their people are their most valuable asset. However, people will make up their own minds as to whether the organization lives up to its stated principles.

- **Talk about solutions**

Emotionally intelligent leaders demonstrate that they are thinking ahead—and thinking of others. For example, if the bad news involves job reductions, leaders should address that they have come up with some solutions—including financial aid, help in finding other work, and other means of softening the blow.

EI Exercise:

Avoid jargon and management-speak when delivering bad news. This can be misinterpreted by your audience, raising suspicions and resentment.

Recognize these traits to identify highly sensitive people

In 1991, after years of studying people using functional magnetic imaging, Dr. Elaine Aron coined the term Highly Sensitive Person. Those with this innate temperament can find it be a gift and a curse.

People with this trait require extra time to process, and if something seems off, they will usually identify an issue to be looked into further. Brain scans have shown that highly sensitive persons (HSPs) have more active mirror neurons, which are responsible for feelings of empathy for others. They also have more activity in brain areas that are involved with emotional responses. HSPs feel both positive and negative emotions more intensely than non-HSPs. A large percent of our populace are highly sensitive people. They are thought to be linked to higher levels of creativity, richer personal relationships, and a greater appreciation for beauty. In the workplace, they are an asset to your team for the following reasons.

- **Greater depth of processing**

HSPs are wired to pause and reflect before engaging. Therefore, HSPs are always taking in a lot of information around them and thinking deeply about it. Since HSPs notice more subtle details in their environments, they are more emotionally impacted by social stimulation and will notice the "pulse" of workplace energy.

- **Emotional intensity**

HSPs feel more emotional in response to both positive and negative events, and they pick up on the emotions of others. They need time to reflect before taking action. Even positive transitions—such as getting a promotion or starting a new relationship—can be challenging.

- **Sensory sensitivity**

Certain types of external stimuli bother HSPs. This could include bright lights, loud noises, social stimulation, crowded buses, quickly flashing movie screens, strong smells, and/or rough textures. This is great information to be aware of if your colleague, boss, or partner is an HSP.

- **Attention to detail**

When HSPs are living a lifestyle suitable for their temperament (which includes adequate downtime, meaningful connections, and time to integrate experiences), they access many of the gifts that their highly perceptive brains and heightened emotional capacity afford. HSPs notice little details that others may miss, such as subtle body language or small changes to an environment. Even the little moments can bring HSPs great joy. Compared to others, they tend to feel events more deeply and for longer periods of time. Because they tend to be conscientious, HSPs commit to doing things the right way.

- **Empathetic, caring, intuitive, and perceptive**

HSPs are emotionally responsive toward the needs of others and typically enjoy one-to-one interactions with meaningful connections. With this heightened perception, they notice nonverbal cues. For example, they might be the first to notice if a colleague gets a new haircut or if someone is upset.

El Exercise:

Find out if you—or someone you know—is an HSP by taking a test online. You can find this test at Dr. Aron's website: hsperson.com/test/highly-sensitive-test/.

TIP 27

Work to become an emotionally intelligent leader

Technical proficiency was once considered the main quality when it came to leadership, but now it's considered a necessary entry-level skill.

If leaders lack the ability to communicate, collaborate with others, and set up a culture that supports staff appreciation and development, their technical skills alone will not serve them or their organization well. In these areas, emotional intelligence becomes critical for leadership. When they lack emotional intelligence, leaders will negatively affect employee engagement, satisfaction, turnover, and ultimately the financial bottom line. The good news is that emotional intelligence can be developed. Here are seven way to incorporate it into your work life.

- Show enthusiasm and interest in your organization and people

Emotionally intelligent leaders are the biggest boosters of their organization. They continually show belief in their work, the work of their people, and the success of their organization. This confidence not only boosts the organization itself but also helps employees stay enthused about their work.

- **Display a willingness to step out of your comfort zone**

Growth and development require that we continue to push the boundaries of what we feel comfortable doing. Emotionally strong leaders recognize this and push themselves and others to go beyond what they already know and are familiar with. They recognize that change is constant and that their success, the success of their people, and organization requires constant advancements and adjustments.

- **Control your emotions when needed**

During times of difficulty and crisis, employees will look to leaders for guidance. Even when leaders don't have immediate solutions, those who remain calm can help their team focus its energies on coming up with solutions, rather than needlessly squandering those energies on fear and worry.

- **Pursue authenticity**

When dealing with an emotionally intelligent leader, employees don't have to worry about deciphering the messages they are sending. These leaders share as much as they are able to with their people at all times. They don't feel the need to hide things from others, cover up their mistakes, or play favorites in their workplace. They treat everyone the same, regardless of their position or station in life.

- **Relate to your people on a human level**

Emotionally intelligent leaders are aware of their emotions and are not afraid to express them when appropriate. They are aware of how emotions affect everything we do and are skilled at reading the emotions of others individually and in groups.

- **Don't let setbacks or failures derail your goals**

Rarely does anything go exactly as planned. Failures and setbacks are inevitable parts of the road to anything worth doing. Leaders expect roadblocks and emotionally prepare for them. They look for the lessons learned. To them, it is all part of their development—they are resilient.

- **Don't get sucked into negativity**

Everyone has times when they are down, feel like complaining, and struggle to stay positive. Emotionally intelligent leaders are not immune to those feelings. However, they never allow them to set up permanent residence in their minds. While they are open to and supportive of the feelings of others, they distance themselves from people who are chronic complainers or constantly negative. The people they do surround themselves with display a positive outlook. They believe that life is to be experienced and enjoyed to the fullest; as a result, they attract (and are attracted to) people who live by the same belief.

EI Exercise:

Push your boundaries. Identify a new goal, enroll in a course (for fun or business), learn a second language that could be useful in your business, or pursue anything else that takes you out of your comfort zone. Write it down.

TIP 28

Figure out the why of your organization

"He who has a why can endure any how."
—Friedrich Nietzsche, philosopher

In his TEDx talk, author Simon Sinek expounded on why some products, people, and organizations fail while others succeed. It has to do with a simple theory based in biology about why we make decisions. We have a primitive brain, or limbic system, that holds our emotions. Then there is our powerful thinking brain, the neocortex, which has language and makes rational decisions based upon facts, data, and information. While we may believe we are using our powerful thinking brain to make decisions, we are actually making them based on our emotions, on the *why*. Most organizations and products focus on the *how* and *what*, but miss the *why*—the inner emotional part of why we do what we do.

How do you explain the success of Harley Davidson? Japanese manufacturers have been making more technically advanced, reliable, and less expensive motorcycles for decades. According to our rational brain, Harley Davidson should have gone out of business a long time ago. But Harley Davidson isn't selling motorcycles; it's selling the experience: freedom, the open road, the lifestyle. People looking for that experience join the Harley brand. Similarly, when you help an organization figure out its *why,* you also help . . .

- Ground the organization and provide direction

Discovering the *why* grounds organizations and gives them a base from which they can make decisions, grow, and evolve. People who have no sense of who they are or what they stand for are rudderless, drifting whichever way the wind blows. This also applies to organizations. Without a sense of purpose, they will have nothing to point to when it comes to making decisions that affect their future. The *why* provides moral direction when difficult decisions arise.

- Attract loyal employees with the same belief

Organizations that know their purpose, proclaim it, and put it out there will attract people to their company who share their beliefs. This has always been true to some degree, but in the past, people were more willing to put up with working for organizations whose values conflicted with their own. In today's workplace, this is changing. Younger generations are no longer willing to work for just a paycheck but want to contribute to something worthwhile, to make a difference. In a world of rapid workplace turnover, employees who identify with the values of an organization are less likely to leave.

- Attract loyal customers sharing similar beliefs

Knowing an organization's *why* attracts customers who want to buy their products and services. Witness the many organizations that promote themselves as green and environmentally friendly.

They are well aware that this will attract customers who will only purchase from an organization that shares their values.

● **Create stronger teams**

People who share similar values and beliefs will get along better, making it easier to work toward a common goal. If those people are working in a company that also shares those commonly held values, a strong dynamic force is created. Such a workplace requires less supervision or external forces to keep everything on track. Instead, staff are internally motivated to do their best, aligning their own personal success with the success of the organization.

● **Provide clarity for focused communication and marketing**

A company's clear purpose provides a central focus for all communication and marketing. Everything that goes out internally and externally can be evaluated against how well it stacks up against that purpose. This provides valuable direction and ensures a consistent message about who they are and what they believe.

EI Exercise:

Write down the *why* for your business. Ask your team members to do the same, to see if everyone is on the same page.

TIP 29

Foster a spirit of giving

"You give but little when you give of your possessions.
It is when you give of yourself that you truly give."
—*Kahlil Gibran, poet, painter, and author of* The Prophet

During the holidays, we are constantly reminded of others less fortunate, and we are encouraged to reach out and give. All major world religions speak to the importance of helping those in need. In addition to individuals feeling good about meeting moral obligations, organizations also experience real benefits. So why not encourage acts of selfless service? Here's what you can expect such a spirit of giving to do for your organization.

- **Encourage new skills and build stronger connections**

While contributing to a worthwhile charity makes employees feel better about themselves, it also makes them feel better about the organization they work for. It shows staff that the organization has a moral conscience and cares about more than turning a profit. Working on a nonprofit project together allows people to learn and practice different skills, experience each other in a new light, and deepen their relationships.

● **Open the door to greater empathy and gratitude**

Coming into contact with people who have a lot less than us increases our empathy—not everyone has the same opportunities. It also makes us feel gratitude for what we have. This awareness may cause us to rethink our relationships in and outside of the workplace. It could lead to more appreciation and to us focusing more on the positives of the workplace, rather than on what is lacking.

● **Add energy and fun, and break up the routine.**

There is a saying that a change is better than a rest. Most workplaces can and do get caught up in monotonous routines at times. The longer that routine become the norm, the more comfortable it becomes and the more difficult it is to break out of the rut. Doing something totally outside of the norm, like helping a nonprofit, breaks the chains of routine and allows people to be themselves, have fun, and feel renewed energy and sense of purpose.

EI Exercise:

Do an informal survey of team members to see which nonprofits they support or serve as volunteers—whether that's packaging diapers for young mothers, sorting and delivering books to school libraries, packing lunches for the unhoused, or any number of worthy endeavors. Select one that would allow your department or other groups of staff to spend time together in a volunteer setting.

TIP 30

Manage your emotions for greater effectiveness

"I don't want to be at the mercy of my emotions. I want to use them, to enjoy them, and to dominate them." —Oscar Wilde, poet and playwright, from The Picture of Dorian Gray

We are all familiar with the increasing attention given to soft skills in the workplace. While managing our emotions effectively in the workplace is a major component for success for everyone, it is crucial for leaders. A leader who is not managing his or her emotions can create severe havoc within an organization, damaging employee morale, retention, and profit. While employees may get away with an occasional lapse in emotional control, leaders are not afforded that leeway. Every reaction, positive or negative, has consequences. Here are ways for you to manage your emotions.

- **Become acutely self-aware**

Effective leaders understand their emotional state, what triggers them, and what they need to do to make sure that their emotions don't get the best of them. They understand the importance of keeping their cool in all situations and not reacting until they think things through, responding from a place of reason.

● Share appropriately

It is not necessary or healthy for leaders to be unemotional robots. Effective leaders connect through their ability to share emotions, which can enhance relationships. Whether an employee is feeling joy over a successful sales week or sadness over a family member passing, an effective leader can mirror emotions as a way to connect on a heart level.

● Manage your own moods and feelings

Successful leaders have ups and downs just like everyone else. Events occur that are difficult to deal with and can put us all in a bad mood. Good managers put these feelings aside for the moment and focus on what needs to be done. They pick the time and place to express difficult thoughts and feelings, aware that others count on them to be focused and supportive in the workplace.

● Overcome apathy, inertia, and procrastination

Have you ever had a day when you felt like doing very little or leaving things undone until later? We have all had those days. Leaders experience the same struggles but do not have the luxury of giving in to them—too many others depend on them to get things done, whether they feel like it or not. Successful leaders discipline themselves to do whatever it takes, regardless of how they feel at the moment.

EI Exercise:

Become aware of your work habits, especially those that lead to procrastination. This may require eliminating distractions in your office, devoting an uninterrupted block of time to a project or finding a new organizational system.

TIP 31

Unleash the power of introverts in your workplace

"There is no such thing as a pure introvert or extrovert.
Such a person would be in the lunatic asylum."
—Carl G. Jung, founder of analytical psychology

What do Warren Buffet, Mahatma Gandhi, and Rosa Parks have in common? They are introverts who would likely be completely overlooked in US corporate boardrooms today. The current business culture seems to value and emphasize those individuals who project "personality" and strive to be noticed. These extroverts speak fast, loud, and a lot. They think *while* they are speaking. Introverts, on the other hand, tend to process their ideas before opening their mouths. In the US and some other countries, introverts have been pushed to the background. As a result, you might not always hear from the person with the best, most creative ideas but from the one who is the loudest. Here are some ideas to for making your workplace more introvert-friendly.

- **Understand introverts and extroverts**

One of the common misconceptions regarding introverts is that they are shy and withdrawn. Carl Jung, who made the terms *extrovert* and *introvert* popular, claimed that the difference between them was how they gained energy. Introverts gained energy from spending time alone. When around others for too long, they find their energy drained. They are not necessarily shy or withdrawn; they just need to get away to recharge

- **Create an introvert-friendly environment**

Organizations can deliberately create an environment that is friendly to thoughtful introspection, allowing introverts opportunities to make use of their talents and abilities:

- Allocate time for all members to speak and be heard. Make it understood that the speaker is not to be interrupted until the end, at which point anyone can ask questions.
- Ask meeting participants to convey their desired discussion ahead of time, and then for the meeting chair to compile and convey them to everyone prior to the meeting. This invites more thoughtful participation from introverts, who welcome time to think through agenda items rather than be asked to spontaneously respond.
- Invite feedback on ways to improve plans and processes— both in writing and in person. Allow time to circle back for more details. Pay special attention to thoughtful and creative ideas, even if unable to use them.
- Give notice of changes and events as far in advance as possible.

EI Exercise:

Take the ten-question quiz from TED (ideas.ted.com /quiz-are-you-an-extrovert-introvert-or-ambivert/), and ask your coworkers to take the quiz too. Organizational psychologist Adam Grant, in his *WorkLife* podcast, says, "To work well with other people, you need to understand their personalities, and they need to understand yours."

TIP 32

Take steps when a star employee disengages

"The simple act of paying positive attention to people has a great deal to do with productivity." —Tom Peters, economist and author of In Search of Excellence

It is one of management's greatest nightmares: one of their finest people has suddenly turned cold. The person who did more than their share, came up with great ideas, enthusiastically helped others, and lifted the spirits of the team suddenly seems disinterested in even doing his or her own job. This employee used to be the first to arrive and the last to leave but recently has been coming in late. In the past, he or she rarely called in sick but now does so regularly. And others are complaining that this once-valued colleague is no longer doing a fair share of the work. As a manager you have to do something. Consider starting here to find out what is going on and what changes are necessary.

- **Don't make assumptions about the cause of the problem**

Your employee could be acting this way for many reasons—some having nothing to do with their job. Perhaps he found a new passion or purpose or is experiencing something disruptive in his personal life. Maybe the work she once found challenging and meaningful no longer holds her interest.

- **Pick a time and place to have a conversation**

Calling this individual into your office could be intimidating and stifle open conversation. Find a place that will be more comfortable. Pick a time when there are no looming deadlines or work that requires a high level of focus.

- **Be firm but sensitive**

This is where having a high degree of emotional intelligence becomes so crucial for you as a manager. Start the conversation by talking about past positive performance—about concrete successes and ways your team member has gone over and above what was expected. Then mention what you have observed and the changes you have seen. Never make interpretations or assumptions about what has caused this change in behavior; leave that up to the individual to explain. In this critical conversation, use open-ended questions, comments, and statements.

- **Practice active listening**

At this point, remind yourself that you are simply trying to discern what is going on. To do this you have to actively listen. To make sure you have heard correctly, repeat what you have heard, asking for explanations of anything you aren't clear about. Wait a few seconds before responding, to confirm that you are taking what he or she said seriously. This pause also gives your team member the opportunity for self-reflection and possible further outpouring of information or personal revelation.

- **Come up with a joint plan to resolve the issues**

Ask what he or she needs from the organization to help turn things around. Do the same for challenges tied to the individual's personal life. Don't assume you have to respond on the spot; ask to circle back later with ideas. But don't make promises that you cannot realistically follow through on.

- **Or make the departure a win/win**

If it turns out that this team member's interests, passions, or future plans no longer align with that of the organization, thank him or her for all past contributions and offer your blessing for the future. Do whatever you can to make the departure as pleasant an experience as possible.

EI Exercise:

The worst thing to do is to let the disengagement continue and hope that the employee comes around. If anything, it will get worse and his or her actions will negatively affect others. Have that difficult conversation—sooner rather than later.

TIP 33

Look for emotional intelligence when hiring

The more you can get interviewees off guard and into a real conversation, the more open and honest they will be.

Emotional intelligence involves self-awareness, self-regulation, motivation, empathy, and social skills. With these qualities, someone possesses the ability to work well with others and to effectively lead change. As organizations become more aware of the importance of emotional intelligence, they begin to look for people with these skills. In a traditional interview, many smart people figure out how to answer as if they have these skills, whether they actually do or not. What can you do to get authentic answers? First, take the interview out of the traditional office setting. Go to a quiet coffee shop, park, or other place where you won't be interrupted. Second, instead of the typical question-and-answer method, try to turn the interview into a conversation with questions like these.

● **What bothers you most about people?**

First, tell a story about dealing with a family member or former colleague who annoys you. Your purpose in doing this is to encourage your interviewee to relax and feel as if he or she is having a conversation, rather than being interviewed. Then ask if there is anyone at this person's last job or in their personal life who bothers them. The answer will give you valuable insight into how they perceive and understand people.

● **Tell me about a day when everything went wrong**

You can start out by giving an example from one of your own "days from hell," then invite your interviewee to share about a difficult situation. Did he or she dwell upon the problem, blame-shift, or look for solutions? Look for coping mechanisms and flexibility in dealing with change and unpredictability. Does this individual seem to take responsibility or look to blame others?

● **Tell me about a close work colleague or friend. What compels you two to get along?**

The relationships people build with others tell us a lot about how they see themselves and what they value in others. This kind of conversation also provides feedback on how self-aware the individual is about his or her impact on others. Humor, unless it is sarcastic and demeaning, is always a good sign.

● **What is something you can teach me?**

Ask this person to actually teach you something, rather than vaguely mention a skill or area of knowledge. Even if you understand the explanation, behave as if it isn't quite clear, and ask questions that indicate you don't fully get it. You can learn a lot from this person's reaction. Does she seem to get frustrated or impatient, or does she ask questions to gather more information on what it is you don't get? Does he take responsibility for not describing it well enough the first time, or does he seem to blame you? Some red flags you might look for: frustration and impatience in facial expression, body language, and tone of voice.

- **Whom do you admire most and why?**

People tend to model themselves after those they admire, who share characteristics they value. In your conversation with this interviewee, consider the object of his or her admiration. Is it a people-person who inspires and uplifts others? Someone who has doggedly pursued and achieved success? Those are valuable traits. But push further into the hero's character. Ask if your interviewee has adopted any qualities from this person, or if there's anything your interviewee *wouldn't* want to emulate.

- **What is one thing you are most proud of, and what makes it so special?**

To get this conversation started, offer an example of your own. Then listen. When your interviewee talks about achievements, does he include and credit others, or is he a one-man show? Does she talk about how her achievement made others feel—how proud family, friends, or co-workers were? Is the achievement based on the work of a team or do you get the feeling that this interviewee feels solely responsible for his or her own success?

- **If you owned your own company, what kind of people would you hire, and why?**

This will give you valuable insight into how your interviewee views people. Does she focus on people or on outcomes? What is his style of relating to others, and what kind of people is he most comfortable/least comfortable working with? Do you sense if this person likes to work closely with others or prefers to work independently?

EI Exercise:

At your next interview, be creative, sharing your own stories and experiences to get the applicant to open up and share more of himself or herself.

TIP 34

Get employee appreciation right

"People work for money but go the extra mile for praise, recognition, and rewards." —Dale Carnegie, writer and businessman

Many employee-recognition programs seem to have little or no impact. In fact, if not carried out well, they can actually act as a disincentive. To do employee recognition well demands that an organization take the time and make the effort to find out what makes their people feel appreciated. Consider these points.

- **Remember: one size does not fit all**

When it comes to appreciation, we are not all the same. In *The Five Languages of Appreciation in the Workplace*, authors Gary Chapman and Paul White lay out different ways people prefer to be appreciated. If the method misses the mark (in the way the employee wants to receive it), the impact will be wasted. In the worst case it can serve as a turnoff, making someone feel as if he or she is not heard, seen, or appreciated. The best appreciation comes from getting to know the complete lives of employees well, not only about their work but also outside the workplace.

- Tailor your appreciation to specific results achieved and/or behavior witnessed

The traditional staff appreciation day often totally misses the mark, because it paints everyone with the same brush. The person who has put in extra effort and achieved massive results is lumped together with the one who did just enough to avoid getting fired. The staff member who put in extra effort will likely feel resentful that the slacker is being rewarded to the same degree. This sends the message that staff appreciation is merely a function that organizational management has to carry out in order to satisfy some criteria handed down from above.

- Give timely and frequent recognition

Recognition should be given as quickly as possible after someone has reached a goal, done something significant, or been especially supportive of another team member. The closer to the event, the more it will be remembered and the greater impact it will have. Instead of waiting for a major event, where many people are recognized at the same time, carry out small celebrations spontaneously and frequently. When someone does something that goes above and beyond, have a system in place where they can be recognized immediately. This doesn't have to involve a great deal of expense or time. Handwritten notes, photos with team members to put on the wall, or buying someone coffee or lunch are good ways to show that someone's efforts have been noticed.

- Encourage staff to recognize one another

Often people who are high performers, but quiet and not comfortable drawing attention to themselves, are overlooked by their superiors. Have a platform, either online or a physical message board, where staff can share what they value about one another. This is a simple way to let others know what great people they work with and is an effective way of workplace bonding and team building.

EI Exercise:

It is human nature to want to reward people we like. Therefore, it's easy for management to show favoritism. Take steps to minimize this. Develop a system that allows coworkers to decide who gets to receive special recognition within the group, rather than leaving it to management.

Make space to address mental health and addiction

People who are struggling with grief, mental health issues, or addictions are the most vulnerable in our workforce. A great work culture is one that goes out of its way to care for and about them.

Viewers and work colleagues were shocked by the suicide of celebrity chef, author, and host of popular CNN Series *Parts Unknown*, Anthony Bourdain. The way CNN handled the loss is a master lesson on emotional intelligence in the workplace. They halted regular programming in order to do a tribute to Anthony and allow his coworkers and friends to share memories and publicly grieve. This brought light to the alarming trend: suicide now accounts for one in seven deaths for males and one in fourteen for females. Another alarming trend is the rate of opioid addictions. In 2022, the National Library of Medicine reported that opioid use disorder affected 16 million people worldwide, and 2.1 million in the US alone.

Mental health issues and addictions have always been difficult to deal with in the workplace. Congress passed legislation in 2008 requiring coverage for mental illness and substance abuse. However, the devil is in the details; advocates claim that, in fact, many employees still face barriers in receiving access to necessary programs.

Susan Bartel, associate professor of higher education leadership at Maryville University of St. Louis, researches grieving and loss in the workplace and how it affects productivity. She writes, "If [employees] feel their grief is recognized and understood, they are more likely to contribute to the organization even earlier than they could otherwise." The standard policy of three days of bereavement leave adopted by most organizations today does not send a message that employees will be supported in their time of greatest need. After the death of her husband, Sheryl Sandberg, former COO of Meta, revamped Facebook's HR policies to include twenty paid leave days for bereavement. Policies around addictions and mental health should be generous and well-promoted throughout the organization to ensure that all staff are fully aware of them. Here are some tips you can consider.

- **Clearly communicate programs and services**

The only way many staff in organizations find out about what is available to them when facing difficult issues is by scrolling through their benefit package or union booklet. Organizations need to make more of an effort by putting out information through both social media, regular announcements, and special messaging tied to events in the news. Staff meetings and events would be another excellent opportunity to remind employees of what is available. Links to and information on organizations such as the National Suicide Prevention Lifeline should be prominently displayed on the organization's internal web pages.

- **Promote a visible and active EAP (Employee Assistance Program)**

Many organizations have an EAP, but staff have to dig up information on how to contact them and what they offer. The subtle message: "We're obligated to offer this but don't really encourage you to use it." EAP managers need to be much more proactive, holding regular meetings to describe their services. Staff can be encouraged to share or write letters of endorsement (even anonymously) regarding the help they received from their EAP. Program members should be regularly updated and take ongoing training in areas of grief, addiction, and suicide prevention—especially during national events such as National Suicide Prevention Week and National Drug Awareness Week.

- **Ensure that management visibly addresses issues that arise**

Many staff are afraid to speak out about mental health and addiction due to what they perceive as stigma attached to these issues. Observing management actively encouraging awareness and launching initiatives to talk about and help staff in these areas effectively lessens the stigma. If possible, arrange for someone from management to talk about his or her own struggles.

EI Exercise:

Most HR teams and EAP managers possess tremendous resources of knowledge and information. Unfortunately, these internal resources are rarely sought out, organized, and made easily available to employees. Work with your EAP staff to offer self-help programs such as AA or Al-Anon meetings onsite.

TIP 36

Effectively negotiate using emotional intelligence

"You must never try to make all the money that's in a deal. Let the other fellow make some money too, because if you have a reputation for always making all the money, you won't have many deals." —J. Paul Getty, founder of Getty Oil Company

When negotiations end with one of the participants feeling they have lost at the expense of the other, resentment can build—effectively limiting the possibility of success in future negotiations. J. Paul Getty recognized this fundamental aspect of successful negotiation: the outcome needs to be seen as a win by both parties. Everyone involved must have something to gain and something to lose if the negotiations are not successful. Consider these five steps as you prepare for successful negotiation.

- **Be aware of and manage your own emotions**

Any time emotions take over negotiations—with "being right" trumping the focus of making things work for both parties—those negotiations can go sideways quickly. In this test of willpower, one or both parties play a game of one-upmanship. So when a negotiator senses that strong emotions are affecting his or her ability to think strategically, it is best to take a time out to refocus. The more there is at stake in a negotiation, the longer it will take, requiring more patience. When your feelings tell you that you or the other party are at an impasse, stop; come back when you are feeling refreshed and have more energy.

- **Be aware of the needs of the other party**

Successful negotiators make themselves aware of what the other side needs for a win. They ask questions to flush out what it would take for the people opposite them to come to an agreement. Instead of looking at negotiations as an adversarial exercise with winners and losers, they look at the process in terms of forming a successful partnership with benefits for all concerned. If the other side comes from a different cultural background with different value systems, you must be aware of those differences. If you can come up with ideas on how the other side might "sell" the deal to their own people, your leverage in the process increases substantially.

- **Listen actively**

In bargaining, each side needs to feel heard and understood. Repeat what your negotiating partner has just said and ask, "Did I correctly understand you?" That step forces you to actively listen instead of thinking about what you are going to say next.

- **Share emotions and observations when appropriate**

Rather than being as stone-faced as a poker player, try sharing a few emotions that might help move things along. For example, if you are feeling frustrated, communicate that; then delineate observations that the other side might be feeling similarly. Realize that, like you, the other party will have to go back to his or her own people and justify the deal you've made. Bringing up pressures that both of you are under helps build confidence that an agreement can be reached.

- **Be genuine**

Being genuine means not complicating matters or making them even more difficult by using words and phrases to try to hide what the real issues are. Both parties understand what is at stake, so trying to confuse the issues only adds mistrust. Be open, honest, and direct with how your side understands the issue and accept that the other side may have a totally different viewpoint. If you have a personal stand on the subject, bringing it up will help build trust—the other side will not have to guess where you are coming from. If you personally think the offer from the other side is a good one but you will have problems taking it back to your own people, let the other side know that. Perhaps your negotiating partner will have ideas on how you can make this more acceptable to the people you represent.

EI Exercise:

Using the above tips, role-play negotiations before the actual meeting. Your top staff can serve as the scout team.

TIP 37

Tackle procrastination

"Action will destroy your procrastination."
—*Og Mandino, author of* The World's Greatest Salesman

We have all been there and done that: we know we should be working on a project, but we find distractions surrounding us. These devilish temptations reach out, offering instant gratification and satisfaction. In comparison to such delicious pleasures, the work we should be doing seems dull and onerous—with the outcome somewhere down the road, if at all. In these situations, we have all given in to taking the easy road. And one distraction often leads to others. Before we know it, a sizable chunk of time disappears. Consider these simple habits to help you get the upper hand on procrastination.

- **Tie your immediate task to a larger goal you are passionate about**

We are quicker to initiate work on a project when we feel a positive emotional charge around the outcome—imagining how good it will feel at the end. Even though we can't see how completing the report will have any immediate benefit to us, we might motivate ourselves by thinking about that promotion we crave.

- ### Begin with the easiest part

The most difficult step in completing a task is the first one. Sometimes we assume we have to follow a linear sequence: beginning, middle, and all the way to the end. However, in many cases we can start anywhere and work around to the end. Starting at the easiest part takes less emotional resistance. Once we get started, we tend to get on a roll, which gives us the momentum to keep going.

- ### Chunk it down into small, bite-size pieces

The task will seem less daunting if we tell ourselves we are going to spend only five minutes working on it. Again, once we are into the actual work, we find it easier to continue to focus than we expected. We might find ourselves continuing to work past the committed time.

- ### Seek out the environments you work best in

One size does not fit all when it comes to the best environment for you. For example, students are often advised that to study effectively, they need a quiet place with no disturbances. But for some people, a quiet environment leads to daydreaming and tuning out. Studying in an area surrounded by lots of other people might actually stimulate someone's ability to focus. If you don't know what your best environment is, practice in different ones until you find the one that works best for you.

- **Establish reward systems along the way**

Before you knock something off your to-do list that will require considerable time and effort, set yourself up with a system of rewards. In advance of starting, think about how delicious that creamy double-mocha latte will taste. After you have completed your work, savor the reward. Remember how good and satisfying that felt the *next* time you have to tackle a project you would rather avoid. Make the reward something you wouldn't normally give yourself.

- **Work on slaying the perfectionism monster**

The need to be perfect can become a major stumbling block to starting any project. Winston Churchill summed it up well: "Perfection(ism) is the enemy of progress. When we decide we want to try something new, the opportunity and fear of failure and rejection come knocking." The fear of making mistakes keeps many of us paralyzed and unable to begin. Yet we learn by doing and making mistakes. Think of the times in your life that you failed but changed direction and succeeded in the end.

EI Exercise:

If you struggle with impulsiveness, reduce your chances of becoming distracted by considering, before starting a project, what might throw you off track. Unplug, disconnect, and put a hold on everything and everyone that could potentially disrupt your focus. Set a start and end time and commit to not leaving your work until the time is up.

TIP 38

Adopt the best practices of likable and memorable people

"In general, being likable is more about being interested—rather than interesting. Indeed, a good way to convince someone that you are an awesome conversationalist is to simply shut up and let the other person talk." —Karen Salmansohn, author

Who wouldn't want to be more likable and have people think of them in a positive manner? We form closer and deeper relationships with those we want to be part of our lives. In the workplace, being likable will result in better relationships with our colleagues and increase our chances for promotion. Many people hold the misconception that being likable is something we are born with, some predetermined condition that certain people are fortunate to have acquired. As with all human skills, we can become more likable by understanding what causes people to like us, then making a consistent effort to practice those skills. We will soon be rewarded when we start to see results. Here's how you can adopt the practices of likable and memorable people.

- **Let others know you are happy to meet them**

When first meeting, give your best smile, make eye contact, and open up your posture to its widest position. Use a firm handshake when a handshake is appropriate. If you notice something about the other person that you can sincerely compliment, do so—such as a recent and proud accomplishment.

- **Practice being an attentive listener**

Most people love to talk about themselves and will appreciate people who take the time to listen. Next time you are in a conversation, listen as if you are being tested to see how much you can learn about the other person.

- **Don't let anything distract you when others are speaking**

Have you ever spoken with someone who was distracted, glancing at other people in a crowd, or checking his or her watch or cell phone while you were speaking? You likely felt you were not important to that person. Make others aware that you are focused by making them the center of attention. Face them squarely, smile, and make eye contact.

- **Call people by their names and remember important information about them**

When you first meet someone, repeat his or her name and sprinkle it throughout the conversation. Remember things that are important, such as the name of this person's partner, children, pets, or favorite vacation spots. By doing so and mentioning them at appropriate times the next time you see this person, you will stand out. When appropriate to the relationship, consider taking note of important dates, and then send cards or call on those dates. This individual will remember you and look forward to more opportunities to connect with you.

- **Become a great questioner**

Conversations often die quickly or turn into monologues unless they are prompted by good questions. When someone is talking about an enjoyable activity or hobby, ask how he got into it or why she enjoys it so much. Even if only subconsciously, this person will remember and want to be around you because you are so interested in what matters to him or her.

- **Look for areas of common interest**

Discovering areas of interest is an excellent way to deepen your level of connection with others and increase their appreciation of you. We connect and develop the best relationships when we have something in common—even if we have to ask deeper questions to discover less-obvious commonalities.

EI Exercise:

When speaking to people, pay attention to what makes them come alive. Use those opportunities to delve deeper into topics that are of great interest to them. This will leave them with positive impressions and lasting memories of you.

TIP 39

Consider the good from getting fired from your job

"I didn't see it then, but it turned out that being fired from Apple was the best thing that could have ever happened to me."
—Steve Jobs, entrepreneur and co-counder of Apple

While we all dread the thought of being fired, the event may have an upside. Many people who have been fired have gone on to do bigger and better things. Walt Disney was fired from the *Kansas City Star* for lacking imagination and creativity. Other notables let go from jobs include Oprah Winfrey, Thomas Edison, and J. K. Rowling. In these cases, their employers may have actually done them a favor by propelling them along the path to their eventual success. If you are fired, know that you are in good company. Here are ways that getting fired can help you grow and become more successful.

- **Builds resilience**

While being fired can throw us into a temporary crisis mode, we find that we develop necessary coping mechanisms for the future.

It's better to be forced to leave than trapped for years in a job you hate. Coming back after a setback builds strength, and the experience gained is invaluable.

● Builds self-awareness

Being fired forces us to look at our strengths and weaknesses. This enables us to see more clearly who we are and what work is more suitable. As is often the case, the dismissal is a result of a disagreement with our superiors, making us more aware of the people we want to work for and with.

● Builds self-reliance

Necessity, people say, is the mother of invention. Being stuck in a routine can bring complacency, eroding our ability to think and act independently. When forced to reevaluate and rely upon ourselves, we can develop resources and strengths that will serve us well in all areas of our lives.

● Builds self-confidence

The more obstacles and crises we overcome, the more our confidence grows—we know that whatever happens in the future, we can overcome those challenges too.

● Builds courage

It takes a lot of courage to face challenges, overcome obstacles, and reach your potential in life. One way we lose courage is by not acting when we feel we aren't heard—by putting up with situations that sell out our values. While speaking up and standing up for yourself can get you fired, the very act also strengthens your backbone.

EI Exercise:

Are you in a job below your capacity? The longer you stay in the job, coasting along, the more difficult it becomes to leave. Make a list of your skills that are not being used to the fullest. Perhaps it's time to consider these abilities and move on (before such coasting gets you fired). Pursue your dreams.

TIP 40

Using body language to show your emotional intelligence

"It is possible to tell things by a handshake. I like the 'looking in the eye' syndrome. It conveys interest. I like the firm, though not bone-crushing shake. The bone crusher is trying too hard to 'macho it.' The clammy or diffident handshake—fairly or unfairly—gets me off to a bad start with a person."
—George H. W. Bush, in a personal letter, September 1979

Our words are only *one* way to communicate. Our bodies convey thoughts and feelings, too, sending messages that others pick up to help make judgments about us. We have all come across situations where the words people are uttering don't line up with what their bodies are saying. We must become aware of the messages our body language sends to have the impact we intend. While body language signals different things in different cultures, consider these ways to use it appropriately in US culture to convey emotional intelligence.

- **Give others appropriate space**

Like general body language, appropriate personal space varies from culture to culture. If we stand too close to someone, we can make them uncomfortable and inadvertently signal aggressiveness. On the other hand, standing too far away can signal that we are uncomfortable with them or lack confidence in ourselves.

- **Face others squarely**

In US culture, turning away from others or not squaring our bodies while speaking indicates that we might be disinterested, uncomfortable, disengaged, or distrustful of the other person. Shoulders should be parallel, and foot placement should mirror the other person's stance. Lean toward the person speaking, making it clear you are giving them your undivided attention.

- **Practice good posture**

You assume a "power position" when you sit up straight or stand straight. In so doing, you convey confidence and respect in yourself, as well as an interest in what the other person is saying. Slouching indicates a lack of serious interest or concern.

- **Keep from being distracted**

When you scan the room for other people, take out your phone, or check your watch while someone else is speaking to you, you send a message that he or she is uninteresting or unimportant. The other person might then be tempted to shut down and end the conversation; you obviously have more pressing things to do than listen. Emotionally intelligent people guard against this behavior—aware of what it communicates.

- **Make appropriate eye contact**

A lack of eye contact can arouse suspicion that we have something to hide. It might also indicate a lack of interest or self-confidence. Looking down while speaking can be a sign of self-consciousness. On the other hand, intense, sustained eye contact can be seen as being aggressive. Of course, cultures vary in how they practice eye contact. In the US, people with high emotional intelligence maintain eye contact for a few seconds, then glance to the side for a few seconds (rather than to the floor), keeping the conversation focused and respectful. Never roll your eyes—this communicates a lack of respect in some cultures.

- **Keep a warm facial expression**

A natural smile helps people warm up to you, but if smiling doesn't come naturally, forcing it may arouse suspicion and make the person you are speaking to question your sincerity. A neutral, pleasant expression is better than a smile that appears forced. Scowling or conveying a too-severe expression make others uncomfortable and conveys hostility, eliciting defensiveness.

EI Exercise:

Displaying the right body language is just as important as words and tone of voice. As with any other habit, practice until what you wish to convey becomes natural.

TIP 41

Actively manage workplace conflict

*"When dealing with people, remember you are not dealing
with creatures of logic, but creatures of emotion."*
—Dale Carnegie, businessman and writer

Workplace conflict is unavoidable. Handled poorly, it can result in a toxic workplace, low morale, and decreased productivity. Taken to the extreme, it can result in violence. But conflict is not necessarily a bad thing. A workplace without any conflict may be one in which there is little or no engagement, with anger and resentment buried below the surface. As long as people are still engaging, even in a negative way, there remains the possibility of a positive outcome. If handled well, conflict can be turned into better understanding and a deeper, more meaningful connection between people. Here are some things you can do to help manage conflict in the workplace.

- **Try not to take things personally**

Often, anger and other strong emotions are triggered by something that reminds us of our past. In other words, what the person appears angry about isn't really the cause. For example, someone who recently fought with their partner at home could inadvertently snap at a co-worker. Keep in mind that what the other person is angry about may have nothing to do with you personally. On your part, as an emotionally intelligent person, be aware of your own emotional state as well as potential triggers.

• Ask questions

Instead of reacting to negative emotions, emotionally intelligent people try to listen and discern more about the situation. They ask questions that allow the other person an opportunity to express more and become aware of how he or she is acting and feeling. Your questions might open a pathway for more meaningful conversation and resolution.

• Don't avoid or ignore

Uncomfortable with conflict, many people run at the slightest hint of it, pretend it doesn't exist, or minimize it. Yet conflict will not go away on its own. You must work through it so everyone can walk away feeling better about themselves.

• Practice understanding

Everyone fights battles we are not aware of. Emotionally intelligent people understand that the person they are having problems with may be going through a difficult time. Try to be supportive of that person instead of taking offense.

• Be nondefensive but set boundaries

Emotionally intelligent people feel good about themselves and therefore set boundaries. They are not pushovers and will not allow others to take advantage of them. At the same time, they are ready to listen and lend a helping hand.

EI Exercise:

Be proactive. When you sense that someone on your team is going through emotional turmoil, tell him or her what you have noticed. Ask if there is anything you can do to help.

TIP 42

Handle workplace pressure in a healthy way

According to the consulting firm Korn Ferry, a survey in 2018 indicated that nearly two-thirds of professionals say their stress levels at work are higher than they were five years ago.

The survey revealed the culprits leading to increased stress: changes in technology and workload, plus interpersonal conflicts. Regardless of the source of your stress, consider these suggestions for addressing it.

- **Talk to people you trust**

Whether at work or outside of it, emotionally intelligent people have developed relationships with people they trust—with whom they can share their concerns and anxieties. They reach out to these people when pressure starts to build. When necessary, they reach out for professional help before things reach a crisis situation.

- **Take time to respond instead of react**

We feel before we think. When our emotions overwhelm us, we are in danger of reacting from those emotions. Psychologist Daniel Goleman refers to this as an "amygdala hijack." It takes about six seconds for messages to reach our frontal neocortex, or thinking brain, from our amygdala, or emotional brain. Road rage is a prime example. If we learn not to react immediately, our thinking process kicks in and we can make better, more reasoned, decisions. Emotionally intelligent people are tuned in to their emotional level and know when they need to take a break—to begin processing with their thinking brain instead.

- **Set boundaries and stay calm in volatile situations**

Instead of reacting to anger with anger, emotionally intelligent people know this will only exacerbate the situation. By staying calm, listening, and being positive, they can diffuse tense situations. For example, when they feel attacked, they politely but firmly set boundaries. Their ability to step away from their egos allows them to more clearly see the situation and not take it personally.

- **Identify and name your emotions**

The act of naming an emotion removes some of its power and allows you to get a better handle on it. Emotionally intelligent people learn to identify and verbalize a wide range of emotions. They also have discovered how to keep those emotions in check by taking breaks—temporarily getting away from the situation—or confiding in someone.

- Show your authenticity and vulnerability when appropriate

Emotionally intelligent people have a good sense of what to share, to what extent, and when. They allow people to get to know them and see their human side. Yet they know they don't have to be "on" at all times and can protect their own privacy as needed.

EI Exercise:

Do an audit of your emotions. Start by naming them. (An Internet search of "basic emotions" will give you a starting point.) Make notes of when these emotions have surfaced in the workplace. How did you react then? With your "thinking brain" engaged, how would you react next time?

TIP 43

Combat employee loneliness at work

"[E]mployee work loneliness is . . . observable by an employee's coworkers, and [has] a significant influence on employee work performance, both in direct tasks, as well as employee team member and team role effectiveness." —Hakan Ozcelik, professor at Wharton School of Business study

Loneliness is one of the least appreciated and most misunderstood problems in our workplaces. The term may bring up images of social outcasts, extreme introverts, or people who just don't have the tools or ability to connect with their colleagues. Still others find loneliness secondary to issues such as bullying, disrespect, and lack of appreciation. Some believe we should just "suck it up." Millennial author Dan Schawbel, in his book *Back to Human*, explores the need to make connection in this age of increasing isolation. Research indicates that loneliness may be a larger factor in our health than obesity, smoking, exercise, or nutrition. Try these tips to fight loneliness at work.

- **Encourage bonding over food**

The love of food is universal. The opportunities to connect over food in the workplace are endless. Potlucks provide great opportunities for conversation. People can bring in food from their gardens. If kitchen facilities permit, try encouraging employees to prepare a special dish or favorite ethnic food. Working together preparing meals is an excellent way for people to connect.

- **Offer room for people to share interests outside of work**

Organizations have set up various groups such as Toastmasters International, book clubs, and other interest groups to incorporate over lunch breaks. Companies should encourage and support staff that want to set up such groups, as these activities provide a chance to connect on a more personal level. Bring in an expert to share an activity such as yoga, watercolor painting, or cooking.

- **Take personal time at meetings**

A good way to start meetings, whether online or in person, is to ask everyone to share something they are excited about *outside* of work. This is an excellent way for people to get to know one another, especially with new staff.

- **Set up contests or games that require direct interaction and teamwork**

Initiate fun contests that allow employees to get to know each other better and provide opportunities to work together to find solutions. Seeing people in a different light from who they are during their work breaks down barriers and helps build teamwork and appreciation.

EI Exercise:

Set up brown bag forums where people share their expertise with colleagues while eating lunch. As with contests,
this allows staff to see the diverse range of interests and
skills that people possess outside of the ones evident in
their workplace.

TIP 44

Avoid toxic types at work

"Great minds discuss ideas, average ones discuss events, and small minds discuss people." —*Eleanor Roosevelt, diplomat, activist, and US presidential first lady*

We would all love to surround ourselves with supportive people who inspire us to become the best we can be. Unfortunately, some people out there have the opposite effect. These people have been called many things: toxic, energy vampires, or worse. Our ability to recognize these people will help us minimize our time and interaction with them. Avoid or limit your time around these types.

- **Perpetual victims**

These people blame others for their problems and never take responsibility for their own actions. They attribute their lack of success to others, situations, or events. They see other people's success as a result of having opportunities and advantages that they never had.

- **Chronic complainers**

Complainers never seem satisfied unless they have a person, circumstance, or situation to oppose. They have an innate ability to pick out the negative in any situation and have no hesitation pointing it out to you or anyone else who will listen. They love to hang out with other chronic complainers. These people will quickly drain your energy if you aren't able to get away from them.

- **Control freaks**

Control freaks need to be in charge of every situation. When unable to do so, they quickly lose interest and move on to environments where they can be in charge. They love to find needy people with low self-esteem so they can easily control and manipulate them. If they can't control you, they will move on to easier pickings.

- **Envious and jealous types**

These people quickly voice a negative opinion whenever the topic of someone else's success comes up. Often frustrated by not achieving what they feel is due to them, they become annoyed by the success of others because it reveals their own inadequacies. If you are forced to spend time with these types, never share your achievements or dreams with them.

- **Gossips**

Gossips are in their element when discussing people. Often their talk is malicious, and they seem to get great pleasure out of the misfortunes of others rather than the pursuit of their own passions and goals. They have a tendency to interact with others who also have limited interests in the big world around them. Don't be surprised if they fabricate things about you. By ignoring them or laughing off what they say, you will keep them from wasting any of your energy.

• **Judgmental types**

These people see the world as black and white, right or wrong. They allow little space for opinions and viewpoints that differ from their own. You are either on their side or against them. They often lack a healthy sense of humor. If they do use humor, it is often sarcastic and cutting, aimed at anyone who differs in opinions or outlook from them.

• **Arrogant Types**

Almost every workplace contains someone who feels they know more than you or can do everything better than you. Areas where you inarguably excel, they will disregard as unimportant. Arrogance is quite different from self-confidence. Truly self-confident people do not feel threatened by the achievements of others and thus will not belittle or put them down. Arrogance is a way to cover up insecurities. Being around arrogant people will feel like a constant struggle—everything you do will be judged as less than good enough.

EI Exercise:

Ask yourself if you at times resemble any of the above types. Recognizing the possibility will help you rein in the behavior.

TIP 45

Achieve work-life balance

*Many American workers struggle with finding a
work-life system that works, and achieving any type of
work-life balance seems like a myth that is unachievable.*

Not only are we working more hours than in the past, but
technology also makes us accessible around the clock. Time
free from workplace obligations seems ever more elusive. Despite
these realities, some people carve out satisfying and meaningful
lives outside of work. Here are some of the tools you can practice
to achieve the same.

- **Make deliberate choices about what you want in life**

Instead of just letting life happen, people who achieve work-life
balance make deliberate choices about what they want from life
and how they want to spend their time. They talk to their partners, spouses, and others who are important in their lives and
come up with a road map of personal priorities and how they
want to spend their time.

- **Regularly communicate about what is working and what is not**

Work-life balance usually goes off the rails when we let things slide, instead of making intentional choices. People who are good at staying on track choose to continually talk to the important people in their lives about what is working or not and make decisions to change direction if needed.

- **Set aside time for family, friends, and important interests**

People who have managed to carve out a work-life balance don't just wait to see what time is left over after work. They preplan and book time off to spend outside of work, and then they powerfully guard this time. While emergencies happen and situations come up that need their attention at work, they strongly resist unnecessary intrusions on this time.

- **Set parameters around success**

People who manage work-life balance have developed a strong sense of who they are, their values, and what is important to them. Using this as a guideline for everything they do helps them determine what success means to them. They know what makes them happy and strive to get more of that in their lives. While their time may be seen by others as skewed toward either work or life, it is what *they* consider balanced that works for them.

- **Turn off distractions**

People who maintain balance are able to turn off their electronic devices to enjoy uninterrupted time doing what they enjoy. They realize that multi-tasking is a myth. Instead, they focus on the task at hand—seeking out moments to simply enjoy each experience and savor life. Often they have discovered meditation, music, physical activity, or some other interest that allows them to get away from the pressures of everyday life.

El Exercise:

Build your life plan to align with different stages of your life. For example, many entrepreneurs invest a substantial amount of time on the job during the early part of building their businesses. They see this as a sacrifice that will allow them to spend extra time and energy in other areas they are passionate about once the business is established.

TIP 46

Know what never to share at work

Even in the most open environments, consider the limitations on what you should and should not share.

Sharing personal information in the workplace can be confusing. On one hand, we want to develop close relationships with our coworkers and bosses, and being open to sharing ourselves can lessen the distance between them and us. If we share too little, we can be perceived as cold or unfriendly. Yet sharing too much or the wrong kind of information can lead to mistrust, negative judgments, and alienation. Determining what to share depends on accurately assessing your work environment. If your work environment is highly structured and work-oriented, the less personal information shared, the better. On the other hand, if people are open and seem to enjoy sharing their personal lives, they're more likely to expect you to follow suit. Look at those who are most respected in your workplace. Notice how much and what they share and follow their lead. In any case, here is a list of things never to share.

- **Personal information that might be viewed as a negative**

Never share problems you are having with your in-laws or other relationships, your own or your family's struggle with addictions, or any kind of situation that can cause others to see you in a negative light. Financial problems or past criminal activities should be kept strictly to yourself. Your colleagues and boss may view the activities of those in your circle as a reflection on your judgment or character.

- **Negative judgments about others' competence**

There will always be people at work whom you feel are incompetent. For your own well-being, do not broadcast this to your boss or colleagues; such actions never put you in a good light. Others may view you with suspicion and wonder if you are saying negative things about them behind their backs too. Once trust is lost, you'll find it near to impossible to gain back.

- **Political or religious beliefs**

Many people carry their political or religious beliefs with great fervor, and nothing can cause more damage and conflict than questioning or disagreeing with them. So stay far away from these two topics. If directly asked, you could politely say that it is a topic you would prefer not to talk about. Even if you do not express strong beliefs, some people will take offence if you do not agree with them. Also, be careful about bringing up world events that have created strong divisions of opinion. If these topics do arise, the safest and most empathetic sentiment to express is your sadness over those who have suffered pain, death, or hardship as a result of these events.

- **Past adventures, sexual exploits, or your views on the sex lives of others**

Anything you have done in terms of your sex life should stay in the past. A sure way to get into trouble is to mention how attractive you find a colleague or that you think of someone in a sexual manner.

- **Dislike for your Job**

While it may be easy to get caught up complaining about your job, doing so will label you as negative and a poor team player. You will also be excluded from the circle of positive people who are more likely to be promoted and may end up becoming your boss in the future. If you really hate your job, keep it to yourself and start looking elsewhere.

- **Offensive or tasteless jokes**

One of the quickest ways to turn off your coworkers is to make a radical, racial, or otherwise offensive joke. If there is any possibility that someone may find a joke offensive, *don't say it.* Over time, people may forget what you said, but they will never forget the way you made them feel.

EI Exercise:

Make a list of the top politically divisive issues. If pressed—and without compromising your principles—come up with responses that show compassion and understanding for all involved.

TIP 47

Show emotional intelligence during a job interview

"It is never too late to be what you might have been."
—Attributed to George Eliot, novelist and poet

While companies are now working to recruit and hire people with emotional intelligence, there has been less attention paid to how applicants can demonstrate that they possess these competencies. Consider these ways to demonstrate your emotional intelligence in a job interview.

• Actively listen

Instead of focusing on a response to the question being asked, give all your attention to the question itself. Don't give in to the urge to answer the question immediately. Interviewers are looking for a thoughtful response instead of an immediate one that indicates that you are giving a rehearsed answer. Repeat the question in your own words to make sure you understand it the way it was intended.

- **Show positive emotion**

Many interviewees, due to nervousness, come across as wooden and tightly controlled. It's not only OK to show some emotion, but the right emotions will form a connection between the interviewer and you. Try to smile and show authentic enthusiasm. However, if the interviewer gets a whiff that you are coming across as someone other than yourself, they might mistrust you, which would decrease your chances of getting the job.

- **Learn how to answer: What are you most proud of?**

Take a cue from professional athletes when they are interviewed after a win or achievement: they always credit their teammates rather than take personal accolades. When asked about a project you are proud of, or that was successful, be sure to share credit with the team and others involved. Make it clear that you are proud to be a member of the group. This gives you credibility as a team player, as opposed to simply claiming that you are one—which everyone does.

- **Learn how to answer: What are your weaknesses?**

In the past, we were typically advised to mention a weakness that is actually a strength—for example, claiming to be a perfectionist or that you get too involved in your job. These answers do not cut it anymore. Interviewers are looking for something more substantial. When disclosing a weakness, be sure to indicate what you are actively doing to work on it and give examples of making progress. Interviewers know that we all have weaknesses and suspect that we may try to hide those in the interview. As long as your weaknesses do not raise any red flags, being honest, open, and genuine will help gain trust and respect.

- Learn how to answer: What are your strengths?

For this question, rather than only focusing on your qualifications or technical ability, talk about your ability to work well with others in a teamwork setting. It's important to bring up your ability to adapt to change, setbacks, and work well with coworkers and customers. And be prepared to come up with examples. Perhaps there was conflict within your unit or you had to deal with an irate customer. Talk about how you used your soft skills to effectively deal with these situations.

- Learn how to answer: Tell me about a situation when things went off the rails.

The worst thing you can do in this case is to blame others for the situation. State what happened but avoid casting blame. While answering this question, it is OK to acknowledge some emotions through your expressions and body language—this will send the message that the situation was real and not something you made up or that was of no real consequence. If you struggled, let that be known. What the interviewer wants to know is how you reacted and if you did anything to improve the situation. If asked, be prepared to accept your share of the responsibility but speak in terms of what you would have done differently, looking back. Interviewers expect people to make mistakes, but they want to know if you are someone who learns from those mistakes.

EI Exercise:

Be prepared to respond when the interviewer asks if you have any questions. Do your research in advance. Ask questions about the culture and values of an organization, and what it takes for people to be success-ful there. Bring up any positive experiences you've had with people in their organization or with their customers, making appropriate observations. It will show that you are not only interested in a job but are also looking to see how you will fit into the company. If you are a fit, great. If not, you are better off knowing this and spending your time and energy looking elsewhere.

TIP 48

Work through negative emotions

"Life is 10 percent what happens to me and
90 percent how I react to it." —Chuck Swindoll

While the pandemic was particularly difficult, we'll continue to experience scenarios that make us angry, frustrated, disappointed, and fearful. But it's not the situations that make or break us; it's how we respond to them. Successful people have found ways not only to cope with negativity, but also to use the lessons gained to move ahead. Here are ways to work through negative emotions.

- **Do not react immediately**

We feel before we think, and if we react from our negative emotions, the outcomes are rarely good. We all know people whose angry outbursts have cost them dearly in terms of promotions and careers. Whenever you experience powerful emotions, give yourself time to think. It may mean removing yourself from a situation until you can think clearly.

- **Name how you are feeling**

The simple act of naming how you are feeling removes some of the energy of that emotion. It offers distance from the emotion and allows more clarity. Taking the time to identify that strong emotion gives you a chance to step back and reflect on the situation.

- **Share your feeling with others who will be both supportive and objective**

The worst thing to do is commiserate with others who also hold grievances. After all, misery loves company. While it may feel good at the time, it isn't productive and will suck you into a vicious negative cycle. Find a great listener who will give an objective viewpoint of what happened to cause the emotion. This is usually someone who has no stake in it one way or another. When sharing what happened, try to give them only the data, not your judgments.

- **Take a long-term perspective**

Ask yourself how much this will matter to you one year, five years, or ten years from now. Look at your long-term goals and plans and see how this particular situation fits in with them. Is it a battle worth fighting, or will it better serve your future plans to let things go and move on? What will be the likely outcomes of the choices you make from this point on, and how will they help or hinder you in advancing your goals?

- **Look for opportunities to help others**

Mr. Rogers always remembered something his mother told him: in every disaster, look for the helpers. Seek out those people and join in what they are doing. You will be surrounded with people who refuse to dwell on the negative and look for ways to make things better. The good feelings that come from helping will uplift your emotional well-being.

- **Cultivate your gratitude**

You can focus on what you have lost or on what you still possess. As well, you can look for something you actually gained from the present situation. Remember: you give energy to whatever you focus on.

EI Exercise:

Consider a recent encounter that produced strong, negative emotions. Then put yourself in the place of an outside observer and try to see things from the perspective of everyone involved. Come up with as many possible explanations as you can for what occurred. What alternative reasons could explain the actions of those who caused you to have such strong emotions?

TIP 49

If you have to leave your job

"You gain strength, courage, and confidence by every experience in which you really stop to look fear in the face. You are able to say to yourself, 'I have lived through this horror. I can take the next thing that comes along.' You must do the thing you think you cannot do." —Eleanor Roosevelt, diplomat, activist, and US presidential first lady, from You Learn by Living

Many of us have thought about leaving a job to pursue our dreams—perhaps to start a business or pursue a passion. Sadly, many experience regrets for avoiding the risk. While acknowledging practical issues, we also need to overcome inertia—the inertia that accompanies fear when taking a major new direction. Fear keeps so many trapped in a rut. Here are some ways to overcome that fear and go for your dreams.

● **Look to those who have gone before**

You will not have to look far to find people who have overcome their fear of making major changes. It could be someone in your family, a friend, or a neighbor. They all had to come to grips with the uncertainty. Most are happy to share what they went through. All you need to do is ask. Read biographies of successful people, who likely faced major fears to get to where they are.

• Imagine the end of your life as having no regrets

When people on their deathbed voice regrets, they almost always talk about what they *didn't* do rather than what they *did* do. Think of all your own future scenarios: Imagine staying where you are. Next, imagine taking a risk and it not working out. But then, imagine success after that same risk. How would you feel about each of these scenarios?

• Take small steps prior to taking the major plunge

The thought of taking on major changes all at once can leave you paralyzed with fear. Ask yourself what small risk you could take to help move you in the direction of your goal. Can you start working toward your goal or passion before giving up the security of a full-time job? Or can you help someone part-time who is doing what you want to do? Start pursuing your goals on weekends and evenings; work on the skills and abilities you will need to attain your goals. Anything you can do beforehand to prepare will help ease the level of fear when you do make the plunge.

• Look at it as a learning process

Remember that you can change your mind or change your direction at any point in the journey. The place you end up may not be the place where you started. The important part of the journey is that it involves growth and an opportunity to learn more about yourself. You may never reach your full potential if you are unwilling to take some risks to stretch your boundaries.

- Embrace other opportunities that present themselves on the way

Whenever we expand our horizons, we increase the likelihood of opportunities we would not have otherwise considered—opportunities that would not have been presented to us if we had stuck to our regular routine.

- View setbacks as part of the growth curve that eventually leads to success

Most successful people have experienced failure; many of them numerous times before reaching their goals. They used the lessons learned along the way to help them make changes in order to reach their goals. We learn more from our failures than our successes, and people who are ultimately successful maximize the learning from their setbacks.

EI Exercise:

Think of situations in which you overcame unexpected barriers, building your skills and self-confidence. Remember those times and draw upon the energy and sense of resilience that helped you overcome those situations. Write them down and put them up in a prominent place to remind yourself of your ability to change and adapt to new situations and circumstances.

TIP 50

Always work to patch things up with colleagues

"The highest compact we can make with our fellow is, — 'Let there be truth between us two forever more.'" —Ralph Waldo Emerson, essayist, philosopher, and abolitionist

Workplace conflict causes stress, drains energy, and impedes doing your job to the best of your ability. This is true whether the conflict stems from simple misunderstandings or power struggles or rude and belligerent behavior. The good news is that you don't have to sit back and allow yourself to become a victim. If a coworker has said or done something that is taking up emotional space inside of you, you can take action. Unless the other person is closed off, or committed to fighting or holding a grudge, you have a good chance of making some progress by using these steps.

- Wait until strong emotions have settled

Before approaching your coworker, wait until your emotions have settled down and you can think and speak in a calm tone. Wait until your colleague is calm too. Otherwise, he or she may become defensive and assume you want to continue the conflict. Assure this individual that you want to develop a better workplace relationship and that your intent is to resolve your differences.

• Acknowledge your part and apologize where appropriate

If you have regrets about the way you handled yourself in the situation, apologize sincerely and without reservation. Acknowledge any part you had in creating the conflict. If you overreacted, acknowledge that. By starting off talking about what you could have done differently, you allow your colleague to lower that defensive shield and look at how his or her own behavior may have contributed.

• Ask for their perception of the situation

The person you are having problems with will expect you to begin by sharing your grievances, but allowing them to speak first will lower their defensiveness. This will also be a clear indicator that you are seriously interested in resolution. If they feel they weren't heard the first time, which is quite likely, this will give them another opportunity. Lowering the defensiveness and tone of the conversation will allow both of you the chance to look at the situation in a new light.

• Repeat what you heard them say

After your colleague has finished speaking, instead of coming up with a rebuttal or counter argument, repeat in your own words what you heard: "What I heard you say was . . ." Let this person know you are aware of the emotions behind the words, and check in to see if you are correct. Just letting your coworker know he or she was heard, regardless of whether you agree or not, will go a long way toward finding a mutual solution.

- Give your version, sticking to the facts

When it is your turn to talk, stick to the events as they happened and avoid making judgments about the other person's motives. If your colleague did not show up for a scheduled meeting, for example, talk about how that impacted the other people in the meeting, but don't accuse him or her of not caring about the other team members. Your colleague can tell you why he or she didn't show up. Accusations and judgments usually trigger strong reactions. These can often be avoided by sticking to the facts and giving the other person the opportunity to explain.

- Work on a solution and agreement

Ask your colleague if there's anything you could do differently in the future to prevent the same outcome. Ideally, your colleague will follow suit and commit to a more effective way of handling similar situations. Search together for something you can agree on and commit to doing this from now on. If all goes well, this could lead to a closer and more effective working relationship. If not, and you feel that your coworker is avoiding taking responsibility for his or her actions, know that you did your best. Your practice with this process will help you with other work relationships.

EI Exercise:

The next time you interact with a colleague about a disagreement, keep quiet until he or she has finished speaking. Instead of formulating your response while that person is talking, listen as intently as if you needed to later write down everything being said. Focus on his or her words and the emotions behind those words.

TIP 51

Know the importance of IQ and EQ

Some people ask whether IQ or EQ is more important. That's like asking whether the heart or the lungs are more important. The more relevant questions might be: how are they important and to what degree are they connected?

At one time, IQ was considered the prime determinant as to how well we did in our lives. Psychologists such as Howard Gardner felt that IQ was too narrow a measure of someone's ability and proposed the idea of multiple intelligences. Then came Daniel Goleman, who in his seminal work, *Emotional Intelligence: Why It Can Matter More than IQ,* suggested that something called emotional intelligence, or EQ, can be more important than IQ. Since Goleman popularized the term, emotional intelligence has become widely recognized, particularly in the business world.

- Problem-solving vs. relationship-building

IQ determines our level of reasoning and problem-solving abilities. Emotional Quotient, or EQ, determines our ability to recognize, differentiate, and manage our emotions and the emotions of others. IQ determines the grades we get in school and, consequently, what colleges we can get into. To a great extent, that determines our first jobs. So IQ operates as a gatekeeper. But after that, the connection between IQ and success becomes murkier. Daniel Goleman believes that while our IQ may get us a job, it is our EQ that determines how quickly we advance and are promoted. The argument is that after technical skills are accounted for, it is our ability to work and connect with others that determines our success.

- The power of trusted relationships

Nobel prize–winning psychologist Daniel Kahneman believes that we buy things from people we trust and like, even though we may end up paying more. Studies on the success of sales people have borne this out. A great deal of our success in life stems from the depth of our connection with others. In turn, that connection is determined by how well we understand our own emotions. According to Mike Goldman, leadership coach and author of *Breakthrough Leadership Team*, "The biggest obstacle in the way of our personal and professional success and fulfillment is between our ears. When times are challenging, our emotions go on autopilot and we create disempowering actions and habits. Simply shifting our focus will change our reality and our results." The change in focus, Goldman suggests, requires EQ, not IQ.

- Your IQ is set, but your EQ may increase

Our IQ is largely set by the time we get to our late adolescence. Our EQ, on the other hand, is highly malleable, and we can increase it at any point in our lives if we are willing and determined to do so. The analogy of a race car works to explain the connection between IQ and EQ. Picture the race car as a symbol of us making our way through life. The engine and components are our IQ—what we have been given to operate with. The driver is our EQ. If we are fortunate to be given a powerful engine and great components, then we might assume ourselves set for success. However, the driver (EQ) has control over how effectively these components are used and their ability to work together. We all know stories of smart people who have crashed and burned because of their inability to operate themselves effectively. We also know people who would not score that high on an IQ test and who have not done well in school but are doing remarkably well in life. Of course, the combination of a powerful engine and well-designed components in the hands of a highly skilled driver provides a tremendous advantage. So our success in life is to a great degree determined by how effectively we use our IQ and strengthen our EQ to work together in harmony with each other.

EI Exercise:

Take an emotional intelligence test. Examples can be found on the Internet.

TIP 52

Build relationships with coworkers across the generations

"The job of every generation is to discover the flaws of the one that came before it. That's part of growing up, figuring out all the ways your parents and their friends are broken."
—*Justine Larbalestier, co-editor of* Zombies vs. Unicorns

We've heard this many times: baby boomers struggle to adapt to new technology, and millennials resist loyalty and working in offices. These bromides have been passed around to the point that many don't question their validity. Yet people of every generation are multi-faceted and bring traits and skills that cannot be neatly compartmentalized into age stereotyping. Consider how you can develop and maintain healthy relationships with your coworkers regardless of age.

- **Look beyond generalizations and stereotypes**

Be aware that no generation is a homogenous group. Learn to appreciate people as individuals. Apart from generational influences, many other factors have significant impact on us: family origin, race, ethnicity, social status, and childhood experiences.

● Accept differences and avoid judgments

Instead of rushing to judgment, look beneath the surface of people's words and actions. What factors might have led them to think and act this way? When we take time to learn about the ways another generation was raised, we can better appreciate the factors that lead to a different worldview. Start by being a good listener.

● Look for ways to use differences to your advantage

Instead of taking an adversarial view of differences, look for ways that multiple generations can benefit—valuing both technical ability and wisdom from experience. With a variety of generations, you can take advantage of each other's strengths and eliminate weak spots. This will make for a stronger, more cohesive, effective, and balanced workplace.

EI Exercise:

Reach beyond your own age group. Check out some music, books, and other cultural activities of another era. It will be a pleasant surprise when you show curiosity about their interests.

TIP 53

Learn how to boost your confidence

"There is nothing enlightened about shrinking so that other people won't feel insecure around you. We are all meant to shine, as children do." —Marianne Williamson, author of Return to Love

Most people agree that self-confidence is one of the most important factors in how well we do in life. We are born with perfect self-confidence, but it is eroded by many factors as we grow up. Instead of focusing on the things that drag down our confidence, it is important to remember the things that boost it. Whether you are going to a job interview or a first date, giving a speech, or just getting through the day, there are some basic ways you can give yourself that extra boost of confidence.

- **Focus on wins**

Have reminders of your achievements in full view so you can see them every night before going to bed and every morning when you wake up. These might be trophies, awards, or anything you are proud of. If you have no visible record, write down at least five things you are proud to have achieved and post them by the mirror in your bathroom.

● Articulate what you are proud of

What can you put on your résumé? What did you do that took courage? Perhaps you moved away from your family, struck out on your own, or left an abusive relationship—things that others would be afraid of doing. Or maybe your list includes things you *didn't* do, like saying negative things about someone when everyone else jumped in. Have you gone out of your way to help someone when others might not have? List these things and read them whenever you face a situation where you need all your confidence.

● Always give your best

Positive internal dialogue is what Oprah took as the legacy of her third-grade experience: "Time after time, the message was the same: 'If you do your best you will succeed and be valued.'" Give your best in all situations. The outcome may not be what you wanted but you will come away a stronger person, feeling good about yourself. Stand up for what you believe in, what is right. Defend someone who is weaker, someone who is being bullied or treated unfairly. Resist the urge to go along just to get along. Be true to yourself, and you will respect yourself and earn respect from those who matter.

● Keep building your wins

Don't get into comparing your wins with those of others. Your achievement is as important as anyone else's. Only share what you are doing with those who totally support you. Confidence builds upon itself. The more you think you can do, the more you will attempt.

EI Exercise:

Get into the habit of pushing your comfort zone. Keep track of something every week, every month that required courage. It doesn't have to be big. Review the list every so often or before that big date, interview, or event that is going to demand all the confidence you can muster.

Look at failure the emotionally intelligent way

Stephen King threw the manuscript of Carrie *into the garbage after being rejected by thirty publishers. Fortunately, his wife took it out and convinced him to keep trying.*

We have heard all the clichés about failure: The only failure is not having the courage to try. Failure is only wasted if we don't learn the lesson. Certainly, Thomas Edison subscribed to the aforementioned thoughts. He claimed that the thousand times he was unsuccessful in inventing the light bulb eliminated those choices and brought him closer to the one that worked. Most successful people would agree with Edison. They tend to see failure as a source of information, a lesson to learn from that will bring them closer to their goal.

- View failure as a badge of honor

For those who eventually succeed, failure is viewed as a rite of passage, a sort of "paying of dues." Highly successful people seem quite fond of trotting out their prior failures whenever they have a public audience—almost as if their failures are the scars of battle, the price of admission to an exclusive club.

● Dare to fail greatly

Your courage to keep going despite repeated setbacks will bring you to a place of great honor. The same theme is deeply embedded in the American psyche. Theodore Roosevelt, who embodied this spirit, delivered what can be considered a call to action in his 1910 speech at the Sorbonne in Paris:

It is not the critic who counts; not the man who points out how the strong man stumbles or where the doer of deeds could have done them better. The credit belongs to the man who is actually in the arena, whose face is marred by dust and sweat and blood; who strives valiantly; who errs, who comes up short again and again, because there is no effort without error and shortcoming; but who does actually strive to do the deeds; who knows the great enthusiasms, the great devotions; who spends himself in a worthy cause; who at the best knows in the end the triumph of high achievement, and who at the worst, if he fails, at least fails while daring greatly, so that his place shall never be with those cold and timid souls who neither know victory nor defeat.

● Know that the journey is long

We are enamored by the success of those who make it big, yet we generally don't spend a great deal of time thinking about their failures and their arduous journey prior to that achievement. Apart from lottery winners, few people achieve instant success with little effort. Perhaps that is why most successful people feel the need to let us know that it took countless attempts to navigate their way to the destination.

El Exercise:

For insight and motivation to continue your road to achievement, read a biography of someone who overcame great obstacles en route to success. Here are seven recommended books:

- *The Animated Man: A Life of Walt Disney*, Michael Barrier;
- *American Icon: Alan Mulally and the Fight to Save Ford Motor Company*, Bryce G. Hoffman;
- *Educated: A Memoir*, Tara Westover;
- *Me, Myself and Bob: A True Story about Dreams, God, and Talking Vegetables*, Paul Vischer;
- *Up from Slavery*, Booker T. Washington;
- *I'd Like the World to Buy a Coke: The Life and Leadership of Roberto Goizueta*, David Greising; and
- *Alibaba: The House That Jack Ma Built*, Duncan Clark.

TIP 55

Become a better listener

"The most basic of all human needs is the need to understand and be understood. The best way to understand people is to listen to them." —Ralph G. Nichols, author of Are You Listening?

We tend to pay a great deal of attention to our ability to speak. Groups like Toastmasters even declare public speaking an essential ability for those who desire to advance their career. In all the noise concerning the importance of speaking, listening is virtually ignored. Yet we all desire to be heard and understood, and when people provide us with those opportunities, we reward them with our trust and loyalty. Here are three ways you can increase your listening abilities.

- **Be fully in the moment**

When someone is speaking, you must be fully present and in the moment. If another matter urgently demands your attention, politely excuse yourself. Do what you need to and then let the individual know that you are now ready to listen. Pay attention not only to words but also to tone of voice, facial expressions, and body language. This will give you information just as important as the words being spoken. A good way to let someone know you are paying attention is to let that person know that you are aware of their emotional state. You can say things like, "You look worried" or "agitated" or "really relaxed."

- **Put yourself in the other person's shoes**

Whether you agree with the speaker or even have an interest in the topic, try to understand where she is coming from and why. Imagine what his life is like and the struggles he might be facing. People will appreciate that you made the effort to understand and really hear them.

- **Look for and reiterate key points**

Many people have trouble focusing on what someone is saying, especially if they speak for longer than a minute or so. It is easy for our attention to drift. If that's the case, try to pick up a few key points. After the individual finishes, mention the key points; then ask for clarification of anything you did not catch or understand. You will be forgiven for not being able to follow the whole conversation if the speaker believes you made an honest effort.

EI Exercise:

Put yourself in situations that force close listening. Speaking with recent immigrants, for example, requires acute attention because of their accents. Learning another language is another great way to force us to focus and practice active listening.

TIP 56

Talk to strangers to boost your emotional intelligence

In a series of experiments, Nick Epley, professor of behavioral science at the University of Chicago, found that people who reached out to connect with strangers for a few minutes boosted people's level of happiness.

Epley found this boost in happiness to be true regardless of whether the people reaching out considered themselves extroverts or introverts. Why? Humans are social creatures who are hardwired for connection. Yet sometimes we don't reach out to others for fear of rejection; we tell ourselves that others don't want to participate and therefore they will reject us. This assumption rarely turns out to be true. Not only does connecting with strangers help us feel better, but it also increases our emotional intelligence. The other person might welcome the opportunity to interact if we take the initiative. Here are some ways you might increase your emotional intelligence by talking to strangers.

- **Challenge your assumptions**

We often make judgments about others based on their appearance and demeanor. That person who seems grouchy and self-absorbed may not be that way at all. But we'll never know if we don't reach out.

- **Increase your listening skills**

The best way to talk to strangers is to ask for their opinion on a matter, rather than just something that can be answered in a factual manner. People love to give their opinions. We can practice our listening skills by focusing on what they say and delving further into why they think or feel the way they do.

- **Increase empathy**

Reaching out to others not only increases our self-awareness and communication and listening skills, but it also boosts our empathy. Showing an interest in the lives of others, even in a limited way, elevates our awareness of the struggles they may be going through. It decreases feelings of isolation and increases our sense that we are part of something beyond our own immediate needs and interests. Most people are fighting battles. Making contact with strangers helps increase our compassion.

El Exercise:

The next time you're standing in line at the grocery store, elevator, train stop, or a sporting event, ask the person next to you an open-ended question. The more difficult you find the idea of talking to strangers, the more you might work to expand your comfort zone.

TIP 57

Think of networking as a first date

"The mark of a good conversationalist is not that you can talk a lot. The mark is that you can get others to talk a lot. Thus, good schmoozers are good listeners, not good talkers." —Guy Kawasaki, marketer and venture capitalist, from "The Art of Schmoozing"

We have been taught that we need to network to be successful. But many of us hate networking, seeing it as a stressful event in which we have limited time and opportunities to connect and pitch our ideas or products. What if there were a way to turn this around and make networking an event without that pressure, stress, and dread? What if we looked at it as a first date? The healthy way to go into a date is to have fun and find out about the other person. Which may lead to more opportunities. Keep these first-date tips in mind at your next networking event.

- Find out about the other person

One purpose of the first date is to find out as much about the other person as possible to determine if there is compatibility. If there isn't, you can both go forward looking for someone more suitable. Be prepared by having in mind a list of qualities that would determine suitability. Not everyone will be a good match. Don't take rejection personally but continue to put yourself out there. The more you do so, the easier the networking process will become and the better questions you will ask.

- **Ask open-ended questions and really listen**

Everyone has a need to be heard and understood. Once they feel that you are doing that, you will have made a strong connection. The problem is that most people are formulating what they want to say instead of listening closely. Listen completely without even thinking of your response. Repeat in your own words what you heard the person say. Ask questions that will encourage him or her to go deeper into the subject. Everyone you meet at a networking event will be expecting a pitch from you. When they realize you are actually listening, they will be more likely to open up and give you information they wouldn't otherwise offer.

- **Think about what you can offer**

As in any reciprocal relationship, it is always better to offer something before asking for something. Before going to a networking event, consider what you have to offer and continue to focus on that aspect when speaking to people.

- **Focus on building the relationship**

In the first encounter, don't stress yourself out by looking for openings to pitch yourself or your product. Take a long-term view. Work on making a strong connection; your chances of succeeding at a later date increase. What you are doing is laying the foundation for a relationship.

- Take opportunities to show vulnerability and authenticity

Do you feel pressured to be perfect in order to impress the other person so they will want to do business with you? The other party may feel the same way, stifling real conversation and your ability to get to know each other. That doesn't mean you should share all your insecurities and fears. However, by showing you have fears and doubts like everyone else, you lower the pressure level, allowing the other party to show more of their true selves to you. At this level, real connection can occur.

EI Exercise:

As you consider your next networking opportunity, draw up a list of qualities you want to find out about people— qualities that would make great possible connections.

TIP 58

Lean on your emotional intelligence when struggling in a new job

"Learning the ropes" is the most challenging part of a new job and on top of that, there is the added stress of getting to know your new boss and coworkers.

Starting a new job produces a mixture of feelings: excitement together with nervousness. It's like the first day in a new school where everyone knows everyone else. You can feel challenged, even overwhelmed at times. However, employ these strategies to help navigate these times more effectively, lower stress levels, and make the most of this season.

- **Identify and manage your feelings**

Feelings of uncertainty are normal. Every single person you are working with has likely had the same mixture of emotions when they first started working there. Self-awareness allows you to slow down and take your time to get a better sense of a situation. Know that discomfort and some difficulties naturally come with learning a new job.

- **Connect with others**

Trying to form relationships with new people at work can feel like navigating a minefield. You wonder whom to trust, whom to approach with questions. Of course, you should be open and friendly, going out of your way to introduce yourself. Making a good first impression is crucial. Also, identify those new to the organization. They are likely experiencing the same feelings and challenges, and you could rely on each other for mutual support.

- **Be proactive**

When grappling with expectations in a new job, you want to express empathy, ask for help, and practice active listening. Check out what your colleagues' and boss's expectations are and avoid making assumptions about where you do and don't have freedom to use your discretion in decisions. When confronted with a problem, don't simply pretend everything is fine. Ask your boss or colleagues how they would proceed and where they would go for help. Be proactive and come up with suggestions. Remember that the people who hired you want you to succeed. Allow them the opportunity to help you do so.

EI Exercise:

Most people love to talk about challenges they were able to overcome. When faced with a particular problem at work, ask your boss or colleagues if they remember a difficult situation when they started a new position, and what helped them overcome it.

TIP 59

Build stronger connections

"Language is our portal to meaning-making, connection, healing, learning, and self-awareness. When we don't have the language to talk about what we're experiencing, our ability to make sense of what's happening and share it with others is severely limited."
—*Brené Brown, academic and writer, from* Atlas of the Heart

As humans we are wired for connection. We naturally want to be around those who hear us and see us, to feel appreciated and understood. We want to spend more time with the people who make us feel this way, hire them, buy from them, and help them in any manner we can. Successful people build strong networks of people they trust, believe in, and can count on for support through good times and difficulties. Here are ways you can form strong connections.

- **Be emotionally aware**

Emotionally intelligent people are aware of their own emotions and very good at regulating them. They realize that becoming emotionally aware is a lifelong journey and have made a conscious decision to continue to work on increasing their awareness. One way they do so is by increasing their emotional vocabulary.

• Become a good listener

People high in emotional intelligence are active listeners, adept at drawing out others' thoughts and feelings. Concentrate on what the other person is saying instead of trying to formulate your own response. Delve further into others' feelings and perspectives by not jumping to conclusions. Even if you don't agree, you'll gain a deeper understanding of their motivations, which will lead to deeper dialogue and respect.

• Make it about the other person

Have you ever known people who only talk about themselves? You likely want to spend as little time with these people as possible. Emotionally intelligent people do the opposite: they put the focus on other people by showing an interest in their lives. Remember how good it felt when someone surprised you by remembering something important you had told him or her? Likewise, make a point to remember things about others and bring them up in future conversations. You can also take an interest in your employees by checking in with them: provide a safe place for them to express their fears and stressors.

• Present yourself as approachable, secure, and positive

Be aware of the message your demeanor and body language send to others. Your smile, for example, indicates that you are open, welcoming, and positive. Self-deprecating humor in social situations can enliven conversations—making you approachable and putting people at ease. Carolyn Stern, CEO of EI Experience, reminds leaders that "you can be emotional and strong; these characteristics are not mutually exclusive." Stern encourages leaders to embrace their emotions and be human at work. She says, "Time is up for the irreproachable leader who is stoic, detached, and emotionally cold and whose inability to be seen as anything but in control creates tense and inauthentic interactions."

- **Have the courage to show vulnerability**

Brené Brown, who has made it her mission to help others become more vulnerable, states, "Vulnerability is not weakness; it's our greatest measure of courage." Most of us have experienced being shamed and hurt when something we shared was used against us. But by being vulnerable, we show that we are open to the vulnerabilities of others. When people open up to each other, that vulnerability deepens the bond between them. David Cory, founder of Emotional Intelligence Training Company, says, "We get pushback from managers who don't understand why they need to share more of their emotions with their employees. What helps them is to understand that when we share more of who we are, we become known and create the environment for trust and psychological safety to grow."

EI Exercise:

Robert Waldinger, who directs the Harvard Study of Adult Development, notes, "The happiest and most successful people in our eighty-five-year study were those who were actively curious about others. Even when we think we know everything there is to know about someone, there's always room to ask ourselves, 'What is this

person showing me right now that I've never noticed
before? And how could I let them know that I appreciate that?'" Your assignment: When next talking to a long-
time friend, ask yourself the same question posed above:
what new thing are you noticing? Let that person know of
your appreciation.

Carefully manage the "office jerk"

Office jerks can be mean and condescending to people beneath them, but they are sweet angels and the ideal team player whenever their direct supervisor is around.

Office jerks can be found in every workplace. Regardless of how fortunate you are to be working with a great group of supportive, caring coworkers, there always seems to be at least one who makes your work life less than ideal. These individuals look for opportunities to impress the boss and spend an inordinate amount of time speaking just to hear themselves talk. They make sure their superiors know, in great detail, everything they do, regardless of how trivial and meaningless. Not only do they take credit for whatever they do, but they will gladly take credit for your work or the work of your colleagues. Bullies by nature, they look for opportunities to belittle your work in front of their supervisors to make themselves look good. These people have an agenda, and being your friend is not on it. You will never be able to form close, trusting relationships with these people. You have to find a way to manage the situation, not the person—a plan of action to avoid suffering emotional anguish or losing emotional control. To do this, your strategy could include the following.

- **Only offer information that is absolutely necessary**

Remain polite but screen all information you give them. Never give out anything that can be used against you.

- **Count to ten**

If you feel angry and want to lash out at the person, take a few deep breaths or remove yourself from the situation until you have had a chance to calm down and gather your thoughts.

- **Praise other coworkers for good work**

In meetings and in front of your supervisors, recognize your coworkers for their good work. In doing this, you show that you are a good team player and supportive of your coworkers. This may irritate your nemesis. However, complaining will only make them look small and reveal that they are a poor team player.

- **Cultivate good working relationships with other colleagues**

Of course, also develop a good relationship with your supervisors. You will need their support. Likely you aren't the only one who feels this way about this person, and positive relations with others balance out negative feelings you have toward one person.

- **Do not respond to someone's anger or inappropriateness**

If your nemesis becomes angry and verbally lashes out, do whatever you have to, but *do not* get caught up in those emotions. The same holds true for inappropriate comments or behavior. In contrast with your calm, professional response, your nemesis will look foolish.

EI Exercise:

Record any bullying or harassment from the office jerk as soon as possible after the incident happens. Let your supervisor know you have done this.

TIP 61

Carefully navigate difficult conversations

Have you ever had to initiate an unpleasant conversation—the one you dread, the one you would do anything to avoid but can't?

The need for tough conversations crops up anywhere in the workplace: people not doing their jobs, employees missing deadlines, or someone acting dishonestly. While initiating such conversations may never be pleasant or easy, consider this advice to keep things from going south.

• **Have a well-thought-out, clear outcome in mind**

Think about what you want to come out of the conversation. Is it better performance from a staff person, more accountability, or a better relationship with that person? Visualize what the ideal outcome would be and work your way back from there. What do you need to do to move the conversation in that direction?

- **Wait until you feel centered and in complete control of yourself.**

A successful outcome depends upon breaking through defensiveness and having an honest and open conversation. If the conversation starts to break down, if either of you start to become highly emotional, it is better to take a break and start over later. Continuing on after emotions have boiled over will only make the situation worse and decrease the chances of a desirable outcome.

- **Stick to the data**

When speaking, only talk about the facts of the situation. Talk about what actually happened, the effects of that, and the resulting situation. For example, because of missing the deadline, the order was lost, and the company is in danger of losing a customer. Don't make any judgments about why the person missed the deadline. Leave that part for them to tell you. Listen actively when they tell their story.

- **Ask questions to clarify what you didn't understand**

For any progress to be made in coming to a solution, the person you are speaking to must feel heard. That doesn't mean you agree with his or her reasoning or choice. It only means you actually listened and heard. A clear statement would be, "What I heard you say was . . . Is that accurate?"

- **Ask for their opinion**

Ask for the changes you would like to see that would keep the situation from happening again. Then ask the other person what they think needs to change. There is no guarantee that the other person will be open, nondefensive, or willing to be accountable.

However, if the conversation has gone well, the chances of them becoming more open and honest will increase substantially.

● **Do some brainstorming and problem-solving**

Brainstorm solutions, not only for the problem you are dealing with, but also for future scenarios that are likely to occur. Try to come up with a means to resolve disputes that you both agree on. Look for sincere comments the other said, or actions he or she committed to, in order to move the situation toward a resolution. Let the other individual know that you appreciate those steps.

EI Exercise:

If you need to practice, have a mock conversation with someone you trust: a family member, colleague, or friend. Invite them to give you some negative feedback to determine if you are able to remain calm and stick to your plan.

TIP 62

Network to find your ideal job

According to joint research conducted by LinkedIn in 2016,
up to 85 percent of jobs are filled through networking.

Most candidates spend a majority of their time looking for post-ings and applying directly. In today's world, that time would be more effectively spent networking. While introverts may find the thought of networking daunting, their tendency to be well-prepared and good listeners will work to their benefit. With the right strategy, time, effort, and patience, networking can result in landing that job you've been after. Already knowing someone in the company you want to work for helps, but by networking effectively you can find someone within the company who will give you an inside referral. Almost all organizations would rather fill positions internally, through people they already know and trust, rather than take what they consider the greater risk of hiring an outsider. Here are things to consider when coming up with a networking plan.

● **Think strategically about all your social media profiles and posts**

Maybe your friends think photos of your backyard party with loads of booze is cool, but they're not likely to impress a prospective employer. Instead, think of your achievements, awards, and volunteer activities. Do your profiles and posts show someone who is active and engaged with others who cares about their community? What could someone who is looking for the ideal employee see that would make them think they would love to have you as an employee?

● **Use professional social media platforms to find people in your field**

Look closely at people's LinkedIn or Twitter profiles for anything you can connect with. Perhaps you graduated from the same college, or have similar goals or career trajectories. When you reach out to them, offer a sincere compliment, something that impresses you or that you would like to emulate. It feels good to be flattered. Just be careful not to overdo it.

● **Ask a contact if you can have a few minutes of his or her time**

Let this person know that you recognize his or her time is valuable, and you would appreciate a few minutes of it. A face-to-face meeting, if possible, gives you the best opportunity to make a memorable connection. Offer to buy coffee or lunch. An online meeting on Zoom or Skype is the best second choice. If your contact agrees, be well-prepared with questions. Make the time about them, not you. This is not the time to ask about job opportunities or pitch yourself. You are gathering information about them and the work they love to do, and making connections. People love to talk about themselves and their achievements if they don't feel pressured. Listen attentively and look for opportunities to probe and go deeper. Your goal is to make the type of connection that would make them want to refer you for openings in their organization, now or in the future.

- **Always express gratitude**

Even if you've not met in person, but someone acknowledges your initiation with a connection request, always send a reply thanking him or her for that connection. This may lead to future valuable partnerships. And definitely send a thank-you note to anyone who invests time in a personal meeting.

- **Keep the connection alive and vibrant**

A Chinese proverb says the best time to plant a tree was twenty years ago. The second-best time is today. Think of networking in the same way. The sooner you start, the more potential results will come your way. Start networking even when you are not looking for a job. Think ahead and plan where you want to be and strategically network to that point. Keep the connection alive by looking for opportunities to support the people in your network. Do they have a book? Get a copy, and if you like the book, write a positive review and let them know. Comment on their blogs and posts. If your connection is strong, keep them updated on your career. Compliment them on any promotions they receive. Persistence is key. Not every connection will pan out. If they don't, you have lost nothing, but you have gained experience that will help you learn and fine-tune future efforts. Remember that you may be only one well-placed connection away from the job and career of your dreams.

El Exercise:

Always follow up your meeting with a thank-you note. If possible, send a handwritten note. Because so few people do it anymore, it will make you stand out.

TIP 63

Recognize signs that it's time to look for a new job

"Research indicates that employees have three prime needs: interesting work, recognition for doing a good job, and being let in on things that are going on in the company." —Zig Ziglar, motivational speaker

Every day thousands go to work asking themselves the same questions: What is my job giving me? Would I be better off looking for another one? Could I find something I like better? One Gallup Poll in 2013 found that if you don't like your job, you are in the majority; twice as many workers are actively disengaged than actually love their jobs. While you can take some steps to make your workplace more enjoyable and satisfying, there is a limit. Here are major signs that it is likely time to look for a new job.

- **You are in a toxic work environment**

Does going to work every day feel like trying to make it through a minefield—constant negativity, backstabbing, gossiping, and people taking credit for the work of others? Perhaps there's not one person with whom you can have a positive conversation or look forward to seeing. Do you come home exhausted, dreading going to work the next day?

● **Your passion went south some time ago**

Do you find yourself just going through the motions—eagerly look forward to days off or your next vacation? Perhaps you can't get excited or motivated about anything related to work and feel trapped in a rut instead.

● **Your skills are not being utilized**

Has your job become so routine that you hardly have to think about it at all? Does it feel like every day is the same—as if your job could be done by someone with a fraction of your skills and abilities? If you answered yes to these questions, it is likely time to move on.

● **You receive little or no recognition for your work**

Are you proud of the work you do but neither your boss nor anyone else seems to notice? When you propose great ideas, do others just shrug them off? Worse yet, does your boss discourage your ideas and extra effort because you make your coworkers (or even your boss) look bad?

● **You have lost faith in the company and its culture**

Does working at your company compromise your deeply held values? Do you feel as if you have to hold your nose just to come to work? If you find yourself avoiding telling anyone where you work, it is a good sign that you should be looking for another employer.

- Your personal relationships and health are suffering

Is your work affecting your personal life? Do you find yourself arguing with your partner and snapping at the children because you are coming home all stressed out? Have you taken time off due to stress? Do you find yourself feeling down and getting depressed when it is time to go back to work after a vacation?

EI Exercise:

Revisit your long-term goals. Is your present job helping you move in that direction? Have you grown and changed over time and are now looking for more challenges? Have you made discoveries about yourself that prompt you to move in a new direction? Making a change may produce anxiety, yet the thought of never reaching your potential should motivate you to look for another job.

TIP 64

Inject more humor into your workplace

"Against the assault of laughter, nothing can stand." —Mark Twain,
pen name for Samuel Langhorne Clemens, writer and entrepreneur,
from The Mysterious Stranger and Other Curious Tales

Have you ever noticed how difficult it is to spend a lot of time around someone who doesn't have a sense of humor? The same thing holds true for a humorless workplace. Not only is it a place where you don't want to be, it is not the most productive environment. Many believe that humor makes a work environment not only a healthier, happier place to work but also a more productive one. Organizations hire people like Michael Kerr, humorist and business motivational speaker, to bring inspiration while poking fun at their business cultures. Here's what humor offers, which could have you laughing all the way to the bank.

- **Becomes a stress buster**

Humor serves as an antidote to excessive stress buildup—helping us relax and see the lighter side of things. Humor not only decreases our own stress, but it is also contagious, helping *others* release stress.

• Motivates and builds morale

Everyone finds it easier to show up to work when they can expect some laughter. And that laughter goes a long way, motivating us to give our best.

• Builds stronger relationships and stronger teams

It is much easier to approach someone who has a strong sense of humor and with whom you have previously shared a laugh. Humor simply breaks down barriers that cause people to be suspicious and fearful of one another. We no longer worry about harsh judgments for our mistakes, because these people *know* us. When we have a workplace full of people who are comfortable with one another, decision-making becomes easier and less stressful.

• Shows appreciation

In humorless workplaces, even attempts to show appreciation can induce stress. Savvy leaders add humor to the situation. This is why "roasts" are a popular way to give someone a send-off or to honor them. For those who find it difficult to display emotions and affection, humor becomes a vehicle to exhibit how someone has deeply impacted them.

• Boosts our health

"Laughter is the best medicine" is more than just a cute saying. Some studies show that people with a strong sense of humor experience less illness and recover more quickly when they do become ill. Laughter reduces the serum cortical, a hormone released when experiencing stress, and triggers the release of endorphins—the body's feel-good chemicals. A good bout of laughter can release tension and leave muscles relaxed for quite some time afterward. It also increases blood flow, decreasing chances of having heart and other cardiovascular problems.

- **Helps create smoother changes and transitions**

Change and transition naturally evoke feelings of uncertainty and discomfort. Humor helps lubricate and make those changes easier. It takes our mind off the worst-case scenarios. Humor helps form a bond that buffers and eases some of the uncertainty and fears of moving forward. It helps us rise above our worries and assists us to see a lighter, brighter side of a situation.

EI Exercise:

As you consider an upcoming stressful event, take some time to relax and laugh. Read some Mark Twain, stream your favorite comedy film, or watch a few episodes of *The Office*.

Get out of your comfort zone

"Life begins at the end of your comfort zone."
—*Neale Donald Walsch, author, screenwriter, and actor*

The more time you spend in your comfort zone, the more difficult you find it to break free from that space. Many people spend their entire lives there, never venturing outside to see what they might achieve. There is a cost for living that way. While staying inside the bubble offers instant benefits, you end up sacrificing the potential for a better future. Here are ways to get out your comfort zone.

- **Take risks**

Those who never venture far will never know what might have been if they had taken risks. All successful people have taken risks, failed, picked themselves up, and risked again until they figured it out. Going outside of their comfort zones became a lifestyle for many successful people, and they continually do so in their quest for greater achievement.

- **Learn new habits to develop inner strength**

Implementing something new, which makes you uncomfortable, will help you build your inner strength and allow you to continue to push your boundaries. Even if you fail, which often happens, you will have an experience, a learning tool, you can draw upon to help you in the future. These experiences will act as building blocks, which culminate in a more meaningful and fulfilling life.

- **Build confidence**

Confidence is not something we are born with; it is built by setting goals, achieving those goals, and setting more goals. In order to develop confidence, you need to face your fears and then step up and do something you're not sure you can do. Achieving something you thought you couldn't is a huge confidence accelerator—helping you realize you are capable of so much more. The more goals you set and achieve, the more your confidence soars.

- **Become more adaptable to change**

The increased time you stay inside your comfort zones, the scarier new territory will appear to be. The accelerating rate of change in the world today will quickly leave behind those who fear change. For people already pushing their comfort zone, change will not appear as frightening, and they will welcome it as a challenge that opens up possibilities for growth.

- **Foster more creativity**

There is nothing worse for your creativity than never straying from the tried-and-true path. The longer you are unwilling to entertain new thoughts, ideas, and ways of going deeper, the likelier you are to slip into a rut. By trying something new, you stir up your creative juices—awakening your imagination, propelling you to new adventures.

El Exercise:

Imagine you are coming to the end of your life. Do you want to be remembered for taking the safe road or for your accomplishments achieved by a life of risk-taking? Name those future accomplishments.

TIP 66

Learn the art of great conversations

"My music comes from many, many, many places.
My emotions, my feelings, my thoughts, and conversations
I have with people I know who influence me."
—Alicia Keys, Grammy award–winning singer-songwriter

Think of people who seem to bring out the best in you whenever you talk to them. You feel comfortable conversing with them and could go on talking forever. They may be old friends or someone you just met, but the conversation just seems to flow smoothly and naturally. Have you ever wished you had the capacity to talk to strangers like that? Don't despair. Having meaningful conversations is something that can be learned. With enough practice and perseverance, you can become an excellent conversationalist. Here are key ideas that will keep you on the right track.

- **Make it about the other person**

Have you ever had someone talk endlessly about something you didn't have the slightest interest in? You felt as if they were having a conversation with themselves, a monologue, and you just happened to be there. These people seem oblivious to the idea that you may not share their interest. In contrast, the best conversations begin with showing an interest in the other person, their world, and what they might value. Notice things about people and use these observations to start and fuel your conversations.

● Listen, listen, listen

In future conversations, force yourself to listen rather than jumping in with your own need to speak. This is not easy, especially if you are highly extroverted. Show that you listened carefully by repeating what the person just said.

● Move the conversation to a deeper level

Think of the people you are willing to open up to and share concerns. What is it about them that makes you so comfortable disclosing? Likely, they are good at making eye contact and helping you feel like you are receiving their undivided attention. Pay attention to their expressions and how they indicate—with their words and expressions—that they are tracking with you. Their faces light up when you share that you are happy or excited about something, and they take on a solemn, sad look when you share bad news. You sense and feel that they are totally engrossed in what you are telling them. Push yourself to do this in your other conversations. Notice that people will start to react differently to you.

● Allow sufficient time and space

Never start a conversation beyond exchanging quick pleasantries unless you have the time to hear the other person out. Don't ask someone how they are unless you have the time to really hear them. Good conversation requires a slow, relaxed pace and a pressure-free atmosphere devoid of distractions.

EI Exercise:

Deepen your next conversation by asking open-ended questions. Good questions include asking how someone thinks or feels about a topic you are discussing. If you have talked to someone before, ask about something he or she brought up in a previous conversation. Discern what they would most love to talk about.

TIP 67

Develop sought-after skills

According to the 2016 World Economic Forum Future of Jobs Report, emotional intelligence is one of today's top-ten job skills.

Over the last number of years, people have grown increasingly aware that emotional intelligence is an important job skill, even surpassing technical ability. A Career Builder survey in 2011 stated that more than 2,600 hiring managers and human resource professionals found the following: 70 percent stated they valued emotional intelligence in an employee over IQ. Seventy-five percent said they were more likely to promote a worker with high EI. Fifty-nine percent claimed they would not hire someone with a high IQ *if they had low EI.* Here's how you can gain the attention of employers as you work to improve your emotional intelligence.

- **Learn to handle pressure**

To handle pressure and function well in high-stress situations, you must be able to manage your emotions. People with higher levels of emotional intelligence are more aware of their internal thermometer and therefore better able to manage their stress levels.

They've developed better developed coping mechanisms and fostered healthy support systems that allow them to work effectively even in highly stressful situations.

• Become skilled at understanding and cooperating with others

Because teamwork matters so much in the workplace, people who understand, get along with, and work well with others will become increasingly sought after. Highly emotionally intelligent people develop relationships with a diverse range of personalities and people from various cultures and backgrounds.

• Effectively listen

The ability to effectively listen and respond to others is crucial in developing good working relationships. Those who are attuned to a speaker's tone of voice and body language can better pick up on that person's emotions.

• Open yourself to feedback

People with highly developed emotional intelligence will be less defensive and more open to feedback, especially in areas of improvement. Their high level of self-regard allows them to look positively at areas where they can improve, rather than taking the information as criticism of their performance.

• Grow your empathy toward others

Team harmony and working well together calls for staff to be aware of and respond effectively to the feelings of others. People who understand where others are coming from create higher levels of trust and cohesiveness. This allows teams to focus on the task at hand.

- **Set an excellent example**

Colleagues want to emulate someone who does not become flustered when things don't go according to plan. These individuals often attain a high level of influence in an organization, even if they don't hold titles or official designations. Their example of rising above the daily irritations and problems earns them respect from those above them as well as from their colleagues.

- **Make more thoughtful and thorough decisions**

Because of their ability to more clearly see things from another's point of view, highly emotionally intelligent people make better judgments on how their decisions will impact others. This obviously results in better decisions, but these individuals can also do more effective damage control in the case of decisions with negative impact.

EI Exercise:

After completing a stressful project, reinforce team harmony by delivering handwritten notes to your team members expressing your appreciation for hard work and best efforts.

Make a great first impression

"If you want to make a good first impression, smile at people. What does it cost to smile? Nothing. What does it cost not to smile? Everything, if not smiling prevents you from enchanting people." —Guy Kawasaki, marketer and venture capitalist

You may have heard that it takes thirty seconds to make an impression on someone. However, some research indicates that the time interval may be much shorter. A series of experiments by Princeton psychologists Janine Willis and Alexander Todorov—published in 2006 in *Psychological Science*—reported that it takes a tenth of a second to form an impression of a stranger from their face; in addition, longer exposures don't significantly alter those impressions (although they might boost your confidence in your judgments). Here are some things you can do to make a positive first impression.

- **Prepare yourself beforehand**

Be genuinely interested in others and imagine what they would think and feel when you first meet. Consider this information from every aspect—from how to dress to the meeting location itself—to make the other person feel most comfortable.

● **Be self-aware and pay attention to body language**

Be aware of body language, yours and others. Indicate (with your body) that you are open to what others have to say. Approach someone with a smile or a warm welcoming look, and offer a firm handshake or appropriate hug. This is even more important than the words you use.

● **Recognize the importance of names**

One of the sweetest sounds to our ears is that of our own name, properly pronounced. When meeting someone, the first indicator that says they're important to you is how you treat their name. If you're not sure how to pronounce it, say it back to them until you get it right.

● **Manage any distractions**

Nothing turns off someone you first meet more than if you answer a ringing cell phone or seemingly pay attention to something or someone else nearby. Ensure you are not distracted from giving this person your undivided attention.

EI Exercise:

In your next conversation, ask thoughtful questions to encourage the other person to open up and share more of his or her thoughts. Present a warm and nonthreatening demeanor—you'll make it easier for others to trust you and feel comfortable in your presence.

Advance your career with leadership qualities

"We don't hire smart people to tell them what to do,
we hire them to tell us what to do."
—Steve Jobs, entrepreneur and co-founder of Apple

As you advance in your career, technical skills become less necessary because the hands-on work will be done by those expected to possess those particular skill sets. On the other hand, your ability to work effectively with others becomes increasingly important. In other words, your continued career advancement depends on your emotional intelligence—exhibiting the traits that employers have come to recognize as paramount. Practice these traits of emotional intelligence to help your climb up the ladder.

• **Keep steady under pressure**

As responsibilities increase, the pressure and demands upon people increase. You must stay calm and not react to every real or perceived crisis. Those above you expect you to handle situations smoothly. Those reporting to you expect reassurance and support, especially during times of stress or crisis. Even in highly emotionally charged situations, you need to manage your emotions and come up with thoughtful discussion and action.

- **Work through conflict rather than avoid it**

Promotion means having to deal with the inevitable conflict that will come from those reporting to you. You can also expect to witness power struggles and disagreements from those above. In both cases, you must rise above the fray and not become emotionally involved. Instead, look for common ground, mediate, listen, and focus on the bigger picture.

- **Grow in your sensitivity toward a diverse range of people**

Everyone at work has challenges in their private lives that may affect their performance. For example, relationships end and family members become ill or even pass away. Reacting with sensitivity and empathy in these situations can make all the difference between helping staff through their situation or leaving them angry, resentful, unmotivated, and looking for a new job. To grow in your sensitivity requires the trait ubiquitous in nearly every situation: active listening.

- **Admit when you are wrong and learn from your mistakes**

Take mistakes in stride and focus on the lesson learned rather than beat yourself up. That way you are less likely to see the mistake as a personal failure—an attitude you then pass on to those reporting to you. Instead of fearing criticism and condemnation, staff will have less fear of taking initiative and of trying something new. This results in more buy-in, increasing satisfaction and productivity.

EI Exercise:

View feedback, whether from your last performance review or during a one-to-one meeting with your boss, as an opportunity to learn and grow. Keep your ego in check and assume the person giving the feedback has good intentions, wanting to help you improve, as opposed to belittling and tearing you down.

Practice personal traits essential for entrepreneurship

In November 2021, a record 4.5 million Americans left their jobs according to the Society for Human Resource Management in 2022. The reasons vary, but usually there was an awakening, a reexamination of priorities in life, and a desire to find work that was more meaningful and in tune with people's values.

As the COVID-19 pandemic began to slow down, we entered a time now referred to as the Great Resignation. People left their jobs in record numbers. We know from the increase in application for business licenses that a lot of those leaving were looking to entrepreneurship as a way forward. Entrepreneurship may have a glamorous appeal—leaving a secure paycheck to strike out and make a fortune. However, the reality points instead to hard work, persistence, and a determination to overcome setbacks and failures. Not many stories of overnight success exist. Those who do become successful possess mental, physical, and emotional stamina to go the distance. They've learned to take these steps.

- **Develop self-awareness**

As the basis of all emotional intelligence, self-awareness is crucial for entrepreneurs. We think we are rational beings, yet our decisions are often based on our emotions. With a high awareness of feelings, you will use your emotions effectively to make thought-out, well-informed decisions, rather than acting strictly from your emotional space. Self-awareness is also crucial to knowing how you come across to others—your staff, customers, suppliers, and others in your field. Those relationships will have a huge impact on your success. Understanding yourself is the lynchpin of discerning reality, engendering trust, and inspiring people. And sometimes, to gain that understanding, you have to step away from the 24–7 grind and spend time working on yourself, finding the thing that grounds you and brings you clarity and purpose.

- **Exercise impulse control**

When things go wrong, you must control your emotional reactions. Step back and look at the situation from a solutions-based perspective. This often means making immediate sacrifices in terms of time, effort, and finances in order to work toward a future goal.

- **Build supportive relationships**

So much of your success depends on how well others trust and work with you. You need to be interested in the lives of others and know how to treat staff, investors, customers, and suppliers. It's crucial for you to build trust with those you need to make your business successful. Doing so builds the good will you'll need to ride out difficult times.

- **Venture outside your comfort zone**

There is rarely a straight line to success in any organization. Continued change and adaptation is the norm. This requires constant awareness of what is happening in your environment and the ability to constantly push past your comfort zone. The willingness to try new things separates those who start their own business from those who need the comfort of a secure job.

- **Support and mentor others**

On your way to success, develop an attitude of gratitude that makes you want others to succeed. To this end, be ready and willing to provide guidance and support to those on similar journeys, generously sharing in their struggles, setbacks, and triumphs.

EI Exercise:

Conduct a home-base support audit. Entrepreneurship is mentally and emotionally demanding. Do you have family and friends who have faith in you, whom you can count on for support? Running your own business can be lonely and frustrating and filled with setbacks. You'll need as much support and help as you can get.

TIP 71

Develop self-discipline

"With self-discipline most anything is possible."
—Theodore Roosevelt

If you look at high achievers who have made a difference in other people's lives, you will find at least one trait they hold in common: self-discipline. Despite ridicule from naysayers and doubters, they persevered. Self-discipline is not something you are born with, as many believe. It is a set of characteristics we can all develop. Start here.

- **Share your feelings with people you trust**

Disciplined people have learned when and with whom it is safe to share their feelings. Vulnerability is powerful, yet in some situations, your emotions and impulses could be seen as a sign of weakness and then used against you.

- **Grow your self-confidence**

Disciplined people are not born with more self-confidence; they've learned to push their boundaries and move beyond their fears. You can do the same. Just be sure to expect the setbacks and failures that come before a major breakthrough. When you achieve that breakthrough, you'll find in yourself an increase in stamina, resilience, and mental toughness.

● **Choose those you associate with wisely**

Disciplined people hang out with other positive-thinking individuals with whom they share common goals and aspirations. They support one another and celebrate each other's achievements. Negative people are an energy drain. When around negative people, you need to tune out their negativity and limit your interactions with them. In this way, you prevent negative people from taking up your valuable time and energy.

● **Face your fears**

When faced with a calculated risk necessary to reach their objectives, disciplined individuals find ways to overcome their fears, because any worthwhile achievement involves the possibility of failure. You consider the worst-case scenario and, deciding you can withstand it, keep going. Failure is not the worst of possibilities. Rather, missing out on potential achievement should bring you greater cause for concern.

● **Say no when necessary**

Don't say yes just to please others. Disciplined people say no without feeling guilty about it afterward. Develop the ability to say no without hedging your answer or making excuses for why you are unable or willing to do something. This shows others around you that you are not a pushover and should not be approached with unreasonable demands on your time.

- **Don't compare yourself to others**

Do not pay overly much attention to what others think of you and don't compare yourself to others. Your well-defined goals motivate and drive you. Be open to the opinions of others you respect, but ultimately take responsibility for your decisions and outcomes. Your measure of achievement comes from recognizing that you are a better person now than the person you were before, rather than from competing with and comparing your achievements with those of others.

EI Exercise:

Decide what to say yes to. Sometimes saying yes—even if it's demanding of your time—makes sense. For example, serving on your industry's trade board offers networking opportunities and visibility for your company. Working with your favorite nonprofit brings its own rewards. To be able to make time for such worthy pursuits highlights the importance of knowing when to say no.

TIP 72

Develop highly positive attitudes

"If you think you can do a thing or think you can't do a thing, you're right." —Henry Ford, founder of Ford Motor Company

Listen to any motivational speaker, and they will emphasize the importance of a positive attitude. Some believe that a positive attitude is something we either have or do not have. However, you are in control of your thinking and feelings and, therefore, capable of changing your attitude at any time. All you need is the desire to change, the knowledge of what you need to do to change, and the willingness to do the required work. Here are the habits of people who have developed highly positive attitudes.

● Keep moving

Don't make decisions when you're feeling strong emotions but wait until you are able to think rationally and are on an even keel. Force yourself to keep moving and take on tasks even when you don't feel like doing so, realizing that once you get moving, your feelings and attitude will improve. Be aware that beginnings are often difficult, but things will improve once you get further along and feel a sense of accomplishment.

• Believe in yourself and your abilities

Although they've experienced failures just like everyone else, positive people know that to be successful they need to take risks and push their boundaries. Approach new challenges with the belief that you will either be successful or take away lessons from the experience, leading you to be successful in the future.

• Continually set goals

Positive people feel the need to accomplish and are constantly striving to reach new goals. Use your goals to mark your progress and as a way of motivating yourself to stay on target. Goal setting is a way of life; once you have reached one goal, set another one. Having something to striver for constantly adds substance and meaning to your life. Be grateful for what you have while continuing to learn, grow, and accomplish more. Stay curious and always look for new ways to push past barriers.

• Bring your best

Positive people are a pleasure to be around since they tend to bring the best to all situations. Use humor to brighten and liven up events and look for the silver lining in everything that goes wrong. Instead of pointing a finger in blame, look to glean lessons from every situation that has not gone well. Regardless of your circumstances or the conditions of your upbringing, be aware of and thankful for the gifts bestowed upon you.

- **Surround yourself with positive people**

Positive people love the company of other positive people. Your demeanor and energy will attract other positive people. Surrounding yourself with people similar to you has the benefit of helping you stay on the bright side and even increase it.

EI Exercise:

Attend a lecture, read an autobiography of a successful person, or listen to a motivational recording while driving. As a positive person, you are on a lifelong journey of continuous improvement.

TIP 73

Max your happiness

"Work harder on yourself than you do on your job."
—Jim Rohn, entrepreneur

When it comes to research on happiness in the American workforce, the statistics are not flattering. In 2012 the staffing firm Manpower Group discovered that nearly two-thirds of American and Canadian workers were not happy in their jobs. Another recent survey by CNBC in 2022, found that close to 60 percent of American workers were unhappy enough in their jobs to want a new career. While psychologists and social scientists believe that some of our happiness is predetermined by our genes, a major portion is within our control. Regardless of your situation at work, here are ways to maximize your happiness.

- **Give your best**

Happier people believe in doing the best they can, whether or not they are given credit. By giving your best, you create positive feelings about yourself. This establishes character, builds self-regard, and establishes good work habits—all of which will benefit you in the future, whether anyone notices or cares.

- **Determine goals worth striving for**

Work toward clear goals and look beyond everyday workplace irritants and problems to your desired future. Know that the obstacle in front of you will be temporary. View your present situation as a stepping stone, a point of reference, to your destination.

- **Don't get caught up in issues beyond your control**

Happier people don't let themselves get emotionally caught up in negative vibes or gossip—both of which are toxic in the workplace. Instead, they concentrate their attention and energies on the work at hand and other areas in their control.

- **Be willing and ready to help others**

Look for ways you can help others. In 2015, researchers at the University of Wisconsin-Madison found that people who helped others at work were happier than those who didn't. While helping others can lead to promotion, it also leads to better relationships and warm feelings of satisfaction, which helps make the workplace more pleasant. As a result, you will already feel rewarded, whether or not the outside world bestows kudos and appreciation.

- **Avoid negative people as much as possible**

Ditch negative people or chronic complainers at work. Instead, focus on solutions or look at problematic situations from another angle. Your positive energy often causes complainers and whiners to avoid you because they know they will not receive a sympathetic ear. As an unintended consequence, your positivity might result in a negatively focused person changing his or her attitude, at least temporarily.

- **Make gratitude an integral part of your life**

While striving for more in life, happy people are constantly aware of all the reasons they have to be grateful. Express your gratitude freely and openly. Be quick to offer thanks to those who help you or do a kind deed. This attitude attracts people to your positive energy. Colleagues at work want to be around people like you. A related corollary: you can increase your happiness quotient by smiling and thinking of humorous events or situations.

EI Exercise:

If it has been some time since you last communicated with your mentor, take a few moments to drop a note of thanks for all he or she has done to help. Let this person know how well you're doing in your career.

TIP 74

Determine to be resilient

"The greatest glory in living lies not in never falling, but in rising every time we fall." —sometimes attributed to Nelson Mandela, civil rights activist and former president of the Republic of South Africa

Success is seldom a straight road. Those who reach success have almost always taken many detours and dead ends. But with tenacity and determination, they eventually reach their destination. One great example of resilience is Thomas Edison. He failed over one thousand times but continued on, even though he was constantly being ridiculed by the media and those around him. What is it about those who refuse to quit long after most would have given up? Emulate their resilience with these attributes.

- **Know and trust yourself**

Develop a strong sense of who you are and what matters to you. You'll be better able to resist external influences that keep many people from reaching their potential. This strong inner strength helps you deflect criticism, alienation, and ridicule—factors that everyone who forges their own path inevitably face. Make strong connections with others but create powerful internal filters that allow you to block out and ignore information you don't find beneficial. Remember, you are the best person to know and decide what is best for you.

• Find a positive takeaway from every setback

When things don't go according to your plan, look for the lesson. Don't view failure as final. Instead, think of it as an inevitable part of the learning process. Be mentally prepared for setbacks and expect the goals that you set will require a lot of time and effort.

• Take a long-term view

Be prepared for the long haul, fully realizing that anything worth achieving will be difficult and take a great deal of persistence. Remember: your future will be determined by your efforts today. This strong sense of the future motivates you to act even when you see no immediate benefit.

• Cultivate a strongly felt sense of purpose and inner drive

Whether it is a belief in a higher power, a strong sense of purpose, or a great sense of humor, resilient people rely on internal sources of strength to get them through difficult situations. You don't have to rely on others for motivation. You see your life beyond the everyday routine and cannot be easily dissuaded from your chosen path.

• Do not allow uncomfortable thoughts to deter you

Don't let not knowing how to do something stop you. Believe that you will find a way. Have faith in your ability to overcome whatever obstacles are in your path. Expect to find new situations uncomfortable and difficult, but willingly accept this as part of the process.

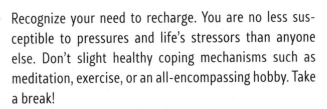

EI Exercise:

Recognize your need to recharge. You are no less susceptible to pressures and life's stressors than anyone else. Don't slight healthy coping mechanisms such as meditation, exercise, or an all-encompassing hobby. Take a break!

TIP 75

Develop persistence

"Nothing in this world can take the place of persistence. Talent will not; nothing is more common than unsuccessful men with talent. Genius will not; unrewarded genius is almost a proverb. Education will not; the world is full of educated derelicts. Persistence and determination alone are omnipotent."
—often attributed to Calvin Coolidge, 30th US president

In any discussion of the attributes of successful people, persistence is always mentioned. Major success seldom comes easily or without great effort. Often the only difference between those who succeed and those who don't is that one group keeps going long after the rest have dropped out. It is relatively easy to persist when things are going well and we see progress. Highly persistent people, however, have found ways to keep going despite major setbacks or evidence of progress. Persistent people possess the following, which keep them going long after most others have given up.

- **All-consuming vision**

Persistent people keep a goal or vision in mind that motivates and drives them. They are often dreamers and visionaries who see their lives as having a higher purpose than simply earning a living. Likewise, your vision should be deeply ingrained. Focus on it constantly and with great emotion and energy. Think of this vision first thing when you wake up and last thing before going to bed to help keep it the focal point of your life.

- **Burning desire**

Never look for an excuse or a way out. What keeps you going is your powerful level of desire. Repeated failures, dead ends, and periods without evident progress often come before any major breakthroughs. Persistent individuals possess the inner energy and intensity to stay motivated during these tough times.

- **Inner Confidence**

People who overcome the odds and achieve greatly are often described as "marching to the beat of their own drummer." Know what you want and don't be swayed by the opinion of the masses. While your inner confidence may be challenged and shaken, it never gets destroyed and constantly acts as a source of courage and determination.

- **Ability to adjust and adapt**

When your plan isn't working, look for better ways to increase your chances of success. Even when you encounter dead ends and detours, have complete faith that you will reach your final destination. Don't be tied to your ego but be willing to admit when something is not working. Adapt the ideas of others that have been shown to work.

● Commitment to lifelong learning

Persistent people realize that any goal worth reaching will take time, effort, and the pursuit of new skills and new thinking. Welcome change and look for ways to incorporate new ideas into your life. View ongoing learning as part of a process through which you continually expand the range of tools you have to work with. Learning and growth do not end at a certain age or stage of life but are the essence of life itself.

EI Exercise:

If you haven't put down on paper your primary goal in life, do so now. Share that goal with someone you trust.

TIP 76

Cultivate optimism

"Optimism is the faith that leads to achievement.
Nothing can be done without hope and confidence."
—Helen Keller, author, disability activist, and political activist

One of the basic attributes of any successful person is their high level of optimism. Without some degree of optimism, we might never try anything new, and our lives would remain perpetually stuck. All advances and achievements in history have been fueled by a sense of optimism. In addition, being optimistic helps make our lives more fulfilling, enjoyable, and fun. While some people believe optimism is something we are born with, we do have control over our thoughts and actions and therefore create our own level of optimism. Here are ways you can boost your level of optimism.

- **Start the day focusing on goals and expectations**

As soon as you wake up, begin thinking about what you want to accomplish, expecting it will happen. Visualize yourself at the end of the day having achieved everything or more than you had planned. Spend a few minutes repeating to yourself your long-term goals, purpose, or life mission. Visualize yourself having already achieved these goals.

- **Each evening, review everything that went well**

Your subconscious mind will go over the last thoughts you had before going to sleep. So spend a few minutes thinking about everything that went right and that you enjoyed during the day just before going to sleep. You'll program positive thoughts and images into your mind.

- **Develop a grateful mindset**

Successful, optimistic people never forget what they have to be grateful for. While striving to reach your goals and achieve more, voice gratitude for what you presently have. Keep a gratitude book in which you write at least ten things you are grateful for, before beginning your day.

- **Always focus on solutions**

Don't waste time looking for whom to blame. Instead, focus on the solution and look for ways to improve the situation. Look at failures as lessons to be learned that will help you avoid or overcome the same circumstance in the future.

- **Focus on the future**

Being optimistic lets you believe that the future will be even better than the past, and you look forward to it with excitement and anticipation. People like Peter Drucker, who lived into his 90s, made it a goal to learn one new thing every year. One year he learned to speak Japanese. Not only does learning support your optimism, it keeps your mind active and open to new possibilities and opportunities.

El Exercise:

Look over your day and make a list of your improvements and achievements. Do this *every* day. Look at life and success as a marathon, built upon continuous small wins and improvements.

TIP 77

Look after your emotional self at work

In 2015, according to the Pew Research Center, millennials spend three times as much as boomers on workout regimens, diet plans, therapy, and apps to improve personal well-being. In their desire to attract millennials, workplaces are taking notice.

When we think of how well organizations look after their employees, we typically think of health and safety areas: ergonomically correct offices and safety committees. However, the area of emotional care is still not well understood and practiced in many organizations. This is changing, led by younger workers whose expectations now permeate the workplace.

• Be aware of your stressors

When it comes to what causes stress, one size does not fit all. Is it the workload, the people you work with, the deadlines? Are you stressed working in a team or working alone? Do you prefer an environment in which a lot is happening, or do you need a quiet area free of distractions? Self-awareness, an essential first step in emotional intelligence, is crucial to knowing what you need to do to look after your emotional needs.

• Know your limits

Saying no does not mean you aren't a good team player. Rather, it serves as an essential part of letting people you work with know that you are at your limit. But frame your no in the right context. Instead of sounding like you are whining about your workload, affirm that you are proud of what you do, the contribution you make, and the quality of your work. Let it be known that if you accept the extra work, the quality of the work you do will suffer, to the detriment of the team and organization. You may find that this will earn you respect from your colleagues and management and encourage others to do the same.

• Block out time to recharge or finish big projects

Set boundaries and let others know where those boundaries are. Do you need quiet time to meditate, recharge, and regenerate? Let everyone know that, outside of emergencies, you would appreciate not being interrupted during this time. If you are working on an important project with a tight deadline, let others know and thank them for allowing you to focus until completion. Encourage others to set boundaries as well, letting you know when they have a deadline or an important piece of work to tackle.

• Ask for help when you need it

There is no benefit to being a hero or a martyr. Asking for help when you need it is not a sign of weakness; it is an indication of someone who knows himself or herself. Others may appreciate that you trust them enough to ask for help. Only do this when you are genuinely overwhelmed. We all know people who are more than happy to let someone else do their work. Let your colleagues know when you have some free time and are able to help them with something in return.

- **Accept all your emotions but chose which you will focus on**

Emotions are neither good nor bad, and we all experience many every day. Instead of wasting energy trying to suppress negative emotions, ride them out but don't keep focusing on them. If you are experiencing positive emotions, extend the positive energy.

EI Exercise:

When you have given your best effort and things don't go as planned, practice being gentle with yourself. Ask how you might use the experience to improve in the future. Look at all setbacks as temporary and not indictments of you as a person.

TIP 78

Find the right career

Surveys show us that a lot of people are unhappy with their work and looking for something more fulfilling. But the question remains: how do we know what we are looking for?

Work that seems to appeal at a distance may not be what we think it is when we are immersed in it. Assessment tools meant to help us make better career choices can leave us cold and even more confused. Many find aspects of work that they love, but others find monotony and boredom; they suspect that fulfilling work is just an illusion. A fortunate few seem to know early on what they want to do and simply follow their dreams. The answer to finding what we truly love to do lies in listening to what our emotions are telling us. Trusting and paying attention to our emotions will eventually bring us the immense satisfaction of finding the work that brings out the best in us. The process might be difficult, yet it's one of the most important journeys we can begin—marking the difference between wandering aimlessly through a life of regret or finding our purpose and the joy that accompanies it. Here are some things that will help you in your search.

- **Let your emotions be your guide**

Your emotions will guide you to discern what feels right for you and what doesn't. Tap into those emotions and use your life experiences to eventually guide you in finding the work you love.

- **Remember that you are the expert**

There is no shortage of people out there who feel that they know how you should live and work—parents, relatives, and friends. But only one person knows you well enough to make those decisions, and that is you. It takes courage and an independent streak for you to follow your own path even if it disappoints those who think they know what is best for you.

- **Find a mentor**

Finding a mentor can help you discern your life's work. Look for someone whose only interest is helping you find the answers for yourself. That means someone who is nonjudgmental, has no preconceived notions of what you should do, and doesn't give advice but asks questions to help you discover more about yourself. Ideally, this individual is successful and happy in his or her own life and has walked through adversity—someone caring and known for his or her service to others, who listens more than talks.

EI Exercise:

Seek different activities. Summer jobs, volunteer work, and travel, become opportunities for discovering things about yourself that may lead you to the right work. The more you are "out there," the more curious, flexible, and adaptable you are, the likelier you are to find something that speaks to you.

TIP 79

Techniques to take charge of your job interview

Confident, talented job seekers know they are in demand and should not be afraid of asking the employer tough questions along the same lines as the ones they are being asked.

Many of us come to job interviews hat in hand, hoping to please our prospective employer so they will hire us. Increasingly, however, job candidates are waking up to the idea that the employer has a need as well, and the job interview should be more about finding compatibility between the two parties than about one coming to beg the other for a job. Job seekers also know that the regular interview process may not provide them with the opportunity to get their true talents and abilities across. In order to ensure you can voice your talents and find out whether you really want to work for this organization, you must have a plan and take over the interview. This requires some tact and preparation, however, so you come across as confident but not conceited or arrogant. If you sense that your confidence is seen as a threat, ask yourself if you really want to work for an organization that would see your abilities and talents as a threat. Here are some ideas for taking charge of the interview.

- **Do your research prior to the interview**

Find out as much as you can about the organization. Websites like Glassdoor are great sources of information. See if you can find opportunities to speak to former and current employees. The employer will be impressed that you have taken the time to find out about them, and you will feel more confident in the interview. Research may also reveal areas of concern that you want to ask about.

- **Anticipate opportunities to bring up questions**

Don't wait until the end of the interview to ask your questions. Look for opportunities to slip your questions smoothly into the flow of the interview and take some control. For example, you are likely to be asked why you left a previous job. After answering, you could in turn ask why the previous person in the position left. If asked what your past employer would say about you, follow up by asking what previous employees would say about their organization. You could ask about the turnover rate in the position you applied for and even overall turnover in the organization. It may not be possible for you to speak to the person who last held the position, but you could ask.

- **Prepare examples of your achievements**

Think of examples of accomplishments in your past job and look for opportunities to share them during the interview. If you are asked about your strengths, share some of the excellent work you have done. If asked about weaknesses, you can segue into asking how the organization supports their employees in their personal and skills growth.

- **Look for nonverbal cues and hesitation**

The reaction of the interviewer or interviewing panel to unanticipated questions will give you cues as to the openness of the work environment. Watch for hesitation, looks of surprise, or attempts to divert or avoid directly answering the questions. For example, let's say the last person before you got fired. The firing might have been based on legitimate reasons, but how your interviewer handles the question could reveal a great deal about the integrity and values of the organization.

EI Exercise:

During an interview, if you're asked about a challenge you've faced, follow up by asking about the company's biggest challenge. If you have done your research, you may already know the answer; be prepared to give examples that demonstrate how you can help them with this situation.

Show your best during a virtual job interview

To be invited to an interview means you already have the necessary qualifications for the job. The interview is meant to determine if you will fit in with the organization.

The whole focus of an interview is to form a positive, emotional connection with the interviewers. While this is more difficult on a screen than in person, you can still create the best opportunity for success. Here are action points to show your emotional intelligence in a virtual interview.

- **Become comfortable with appearing on a screen**

Not everyone is comfortable or familiar with seeing themselves on the screen. If you are not doing regular virtual meetings or talking to friends or family on Zoom, FaceTime, or Microsoft Teams, practice setting up meetings to see how you look. You want to relax and present your authentic self in the interview. Play with the settings and camera angles that show your best features.

Stage what will show in your background, and make sure you are close enough to the screen that your upper body is clearly visible and fills the majority of the screen. Be aware of glare if you wear glasses. Ask others you trust to give you feedback. Looking your best will boost your confidence and help you relax.

- **Practice sharing some emotions virtually with a trusted confidant**

Virtual interviews make it more difficult to connect on an emotional level. The challenge lies in sharing your authentic self instead of appearing stilted. Spend time with a close friend and get feedback on how you come across. Ideally you want to appear warm, open, and welcoming. Smile, if natural for you, but don't overdo it; you don't want to come across as forced. Talk to your friend about situations that bring out various emotions for you and ask for feedback on how authentic you appear.

- **Find out what you can about your interviewers and remember their names**

Whether your interview is in person or virtual, the more you know about the people interviewing you, the more opportunity for you to connect. If you know their names, see if you can find them on LinkedIn or Facebook beforehand. Use this opportunity to learn more, not to reach out. When responding to, or asking a question, occasionally use the person's name.

- **Err on the side of overdressing**

While a T-shirt and jeans may feel comfortable, they are not appropriate for many interviews. Consider the work environment for which you are applying, and use that knowledge to determine how formal or informal, subdued or bold you should dress. Consider covering tattoos, to avoid triggering someone's unconscious bias.

EI Exercise:

Use your background to your advantage in a virtual interview. With a little time and creativity, you can effectively send a desired message about yourself. If the job requires lots of physical activity, show evidence of an active lifestyle. For a job requiring more cerebral activity, sit in front of a full bookshelf. One job seeker discovered before the interview that he shared a love of canoeing with one of his interviewers. As part of his background, he attached a pair of crossed canoe paddles to the wall. You are only limited by your imagination.

TIP 81

Avoid behaviors that will sabotage your career

"If something's not giving you value, consider eliminating it from your life." —Leo Babauta, author, from The Power of Less

You've worked hard and gained the technical skill set needed for your job. At this point in your career, the ability to work effectively with others becomes increasingly important. Employers look to promote staff with emotional intelligence. Show your EI by avoiding career-sabotaging behaviors like these.

- **Inability to manage emotions under pressure**

As responsibilities increase, pressures and demands increase. The ability to stay calm, control emotions, and not react to every crisis rises in tandem. Your boss expects you to handle situations smoothly and calmly. Those on your team expect support and reassurance from you, especially during times of high stress and crisis. If you lack the ability to control your emotions under pressure, you will be overlooked when it comes time to promote.

- **Reluctance to assure others they have been heard**

Many of the problems in the workplace come about as a result of people feeling that they have not been understood. Even if your staff's ideas or advice are not acted upon, you must make the effort to let them know their ideas did not fall on deaf ears. If you lack the ability to make others feel heard and understood, you may well become sidelined when others are promoted.

- **Insensitivity to fellow colleagues**

Everyone at work faces problems and challenging situations in their private lives that affect their workplace performance. People who lack sensitivity and empathy in these situations can leave others angry, resentful, unmotivated, and looking for a new job.

- **Failure to take responsibility for your actions**

People who fail to take responsibility for their actions do not learn from their mistakes and are prone to committing them over and over. They are continually looking for other people or circumstances to blame rather than turning inward to see how they could do better next time. At some level, they feel insecure but cover up their insecurity by focusing outside of themselves whenever something goes wrong. They will, however, be the first to take credit when things go well.

- **Defensiveness and unwillingness to receive constructive feedback**

People whose egos are too large are not often open to learning and improvement. This causes them to take negative feedback as personal criticism. They are less likely to view the person giving the feedback as having good intentions. Rather, they see the person as wanting to intentionally belittle them instead of helping them improve.

● **Inability to manage and work through conflict**

Promotion means having to deal with the inevitable conflict—including power struggles and disagreements—that will come from those reporting to you. Don't become emotionally involved. Instead, look for common ground, listen, and mediate the situation, keeping your eye on the bigger picture.

● **Inability to earn respect from others**

People who are unable to keep their emotions under control, listen to others, and treat them fairly are unable to earn the respect of those they work with. Those reporting to them will not see them as positive role models. They are unapproachable and see their roles as looking out for themselves. When staff see those qualities, they detach from their workplace and put in less effort.

EI Exercise:

Determine if any of these negative behaviors, even to a small degree, apply to you. If so, write down the steps you need to take to eliminate such behavior.

TIP 82

Develop leadership skills in children

"When my mother took her turn to sit in a gown at her graduation, she thought she only had two career options: nursing and teaching. She raised me and my sister to believe that we could do anything, and we believed her."
—Sheryl Sandberg, former Meta COO and founder of LeanIn. org, in her 2011 Barnard College graduation address

When it comes to important positions, parenting rises to the top. The family nucleus has changed dramatically over time, but most parents and other primary caregivers try to do the right thing to raise children to be healthy, happy, well-adapted, functioning adults. Their actions and teachings form a major part of what children will do with their lives. To inspire and help children develop skills crucial to leadership in later life, caregivers can tackle these to-dos.

● **Become an effective role model first**

Children will imitate what they see their caregivers doing, not what they hear them say. Perfection is impossible, but it isn't necessary anyway. Instead, children must witness the adults in their lives expanding their own learning and admitting to and learning from their mistakes. These role models will determine whether children aspire to be leaders or followers.

- Dole out responsibilities and chores as soon as possible

Allow children to take on responsibility, assigning tasks when they are able to perform them. Giving children age-appropriate chores can start with getting toddlers to carry plastic dishes to the table, according to psychologist Dr. Barbara Cox. This encourages children to learn from both their successes and failures. Dr. Cox also suggests that children pack their own suitcases, with adult supervision, around the age of eight to ten. This teaches problem solving and allows them to build self-confidence by taking on new challenges.

- Play family games and encourage team-related activities

One major leadership skill involves learning to work with different kinds of people. An excellent way to develop this is to engage in family games and encourage children to participate in team activities of all kinds: music groups, drama, or any activity where the child indicates a natural interest in. Learning to interact with diverse people builds skills that will serve children well, regardless of what they pursue in the working world.

- Encourage and praise generously but authentically

While children need encouragement and praise, that praise must be merited. Praise without substance, rather than building self-esteem, will have negative consequences later. Expecting the same type of praise when they go out into the world, they will be rudely awakened when they don't receive it.

● **Talk about their feelings**

Helping children identify, express, and manage their emotions is a crucial part of helping them become healthy, functioning adults. Talk about characters in a movie or television program as a good way to help identify emotions and develop an appreciation of their importance. When children have experienced a bad day, encourage them to talk about it. Your role as the listener is to acknowledge their feelings, suggest other ways the problem might have been handled, and brainstorm how to go forward. The child will feel heard and included.

● **Teach them to deal with setbacks, frustrations, and failures**

It is easy to stay positive and upbeat when things are going well. But we all face setbacks. Instead of focusing on failures, praise children for their efforts as a way to teach them to learn from failures—a necessary part of eventual success. They need to understand that failure does not diminish them in any way and does not limit what they are capable of doing. A great way to do this is to tell them about the many highly successful people who persisted after numerous failures, eventually making major breakthroughs in life, such as J. K. Rowling, Oprah, Steven Spielberg, and Walt Disney.

● **Model and encourage reading, lifelong learning, and goal setting**

Dr. Barry Zuckerman, professor at the Boston University School of Medicine, tells us that children who are exposed to books at a young age do better on a number of measures. They have a higher vocabulary, higher literacy, greater concentration, and are better prepared for kindergarten. It is never too early to involve children in reading. The American Academy of Pediatrics recommends that parents start reading out loud to their children from the time they are born or even in utero.

El Exercise:

Set aside one evening as "Family Game Night." Keep the tradition alive even into their teen years.

TIP 83

Use vacation time to boost emotional intelligence

"A wise man travels to discover himself."
—James Russell Lowell, nineteenth century poet,
abolitionist, and diplomat, from "Literary Essays"

Vacation is a time to get away from the stressors of the workplace to relax, regenerate, let loose, and just have fun. The good news is that you can increase your skill sets at the same time. Consider these ways to boost your emotional intelligence during your holidays.

• **Increase self-awareness**

During vacations we tend to slow down and let our minds wander from the pressures of our day-to-day life, noticing things we might otherwise overlook. What kind of people irritate you? What kind of people are you drawn to? Who do these people remind you of? Being in a laid-back, relaxed state is an excellent time for some self-reflection.

- **Increase empathy**

Holidays are a great time to people watch. Notice people and their facial expressions, posture, dress, and manner of walking. In this way, you can gather clues about what is going on with them. Pay attention to people you know, as well as to strangers you encounter in movie theaters, restaurants, and live performances. Ask yourself what emotions they might be feeling, based on body language and tone of voice. Are people around them noticing the same? How might your awareness of someone's emotional state change how you respond to him or her?

- **Increase assertiveness**

Many people struggle with asking for what they want and therefore miss out on getting more from life. When checking into your accommodation, consider asking for an upgrade. Taking the initiative in this way will give you a feeling of satisfaction and increase your self-esteem.

- **Increase stress tolerance**

While we may tell ourselves that we intend to do things like meditate daily, life gets in the way; other things seem more important. Vacations give you the opportunity to return to what you should do for yourself but don't make time for. You can also try new things and stretch yourself.

EI Exercise:

Do an inventory of your life while you're away from the daily grind. What stimulates new thoughts and

aspirations? What gets you excited? If you are going back
to a job or career that is not satisfying, this time could
provide you with the first steps for making changes that
lead to more fulfilling work.

TIP 84

Turn down a job offer if you see red flags

"If you want to be successful, it's just this simple. Know what you are doing. Love what you are doing. And believe in what you are doing." —Will Rogers, comedian and social commentator

Perhaps you've been looking for work or are hoping to get out of a job you hate. An offer comes along, and your first impulse is to go for it. What you are offered seems better than your current position. Not so fast, though. It is not always in your best interests to accept every job offer that comes your way. Instead of moving you ahead, a job offer that isn't right may actually set you back. Before you jump at the offer, make sure you don't see these warning flags.

- **Doesn't move you in the direction of your goal**

People take jobs for many wrong reasons: more money, to leave a job they hate, or to change location. Look at your goals and passions and see if the job will result in moving you closer to your dreams and passions or away from them. It may not be the dream job, but there needs to be a connection to where you are headed. If not, you could be wasting valuable time that will set you back from reaching your destination. When it comes to accepting a job, step back from all of the information, emotion, and confusion to think critically and come to the best answer.

- ### Employer makes outlandish promises

Beware of an employer who makes promises that sound too good to be true and out of bounds for what that organization could reasonably provide. Flattery might be good for our egos, but if recruiters make it sound as if you are the best thing that ever happened to their organization, your BS detectors should go off. Be wary when a potential employer gives greatest emphasis to potential salary or advancement. Question to see how many employees have been able to reach the level the employer is dangling in front of you.

- ### Organization has a high turnover

If you find out that the company has a high staff turnover, your radar should be on full alert. See if you can find out information from former employees. During the interview, always ask about the last person who held the position. High staff turnover could mean a negative or even toxic company culture. If in doubt, check it out.

- ### Organization is viewed negatively in the industry

How is the organization viewed by others in the same industry? Has it been involved in an unusually large number of lawsuits? Customers and suppliers are a good source of information. Do they belong to associations within the industry? You will be identified with the organization, so it's important that you believe in and stand behind it.

• Staff or leaders display unprofessional behavior

Is the potential employer late for the interview? Are people participating in the interview that you weren't told would be there, without apology or explanation? Are they dressed inappropriately for an interview? Are you asked personal questions that should not be part of an interview? Do they call or text you after working hours? Have they called someone at your former workplace—not a reference—without having cleared this with you first? Any of these actions could be the result of poor organization, lack of integrity, or lack of respect for you. Either way, they should raise alarm bells.

• Employer avoids answering questions

When being interviewed for a position, you should not be afraid to ask tough questions such as these: What happened to the last person in the position? What is the turnover rate? How are people promoted? You should be suspicious if there is any hesitation in answering or if it looks as if the employer is trying to hide something. An organization that you want to work for is open and transparent.

• Job expectations don't allow for work-life balance

You may want to have weekends and evenings to spend with family, but the organization expects you to put its needs first and be available at its beck and call. Sacrificing time with family is not something you are prepared to do. You need to be clear about your expectations from the start to avoid getting into a situation you will later regret.

EI Exercise:

Ask people in the community questions about the organization and its people. What kind of reputation do they have? Are they involved in supporting the communities where they are located? Carefully consider the opinions of the community. You will share in the company's reputation, good or bad.

TIP 85

Overcome negative emotions

"Negative emotions are like unwelcome guests. Just because they show up on our doorstep doesn't mean they have a right to stay." —Deepak Chopra, writer and speaker

Perhaps you fear that inflation and recession will jeopardize your quality of life. Worries about money and health can challenge a positive outlook. The scenarios that make us angry, frustrated, disappointed, and fearful may seem endless. However, successful people have found ways not only to cope with negativity, but also use the lessons gained to move ahead. Here are ways to help you work through those negative emotions.

- **Pause**

Whenever you are experiencing powerful emotions, give yourself time to think. Step away from the situation if possible. Reward yourself when you do not surrender to a negative emotion. Do something for yourself that you would not normally do.

- **Name how you are feeling**

The simple act of naming how you feel takes away some of the power your emotions have over you. It gives you distance and allows for more clarity. Step back and reflect on the situation.

- **Share your feelings with those who support you**

Talk with a trusted friend or colleague who is a great listener, especially if that person can give you an unbiased, objective viewpoint of your situation. In talking with this person, stick to the facts, not your judgments.

- **Help others**

You can fight negative feelings by helping others. Many organizations desperately need people just like you to jump in and give a hand. When working with other volunteers, you likely will be surrounded with people who have positive energy—which is contagious.

EI Exercise:

You could focus on what you have lost. Instead, choose to focus on what you have gained.

TIP 86

Enjoy your money more

Those who are happiest with their spending are the most self-aware, reveals a 2016 study published in Psychological Science.

In that study, researchers from the University of Cambridge looked at 76,000 bank-transaction records to determine the happiness purchases bring to people. They uncovered that it wasn't the amount spent that determined the amount of happiness people received. No, it was the degree to which spending matched people's personalities. And this self-awareness is a basic aspect of emotional intelligence. What can you do, as an emotionally intelligent person, to ensure that you enjoy your money more?

• **Know yourself**

Sadly, many people are not in touch with their emotions and have no real idea what they want and what makes them happy. For them, spending money will be a hit-or-miss affair, because they are unable to establish any kind of relationship between what they are spending money on and what increases their happiness. Being in touch with your emotions and what makes you happy allows you to focus your time and resources on providing yourself with more of those items.

• Don't follow others' expectations

How many people do you know who followed their father's or mother's career path and discovered it didn't work for them? The same holds true for spending money. People who don't know themselves well can easily get caught in the trap of spending their money in the same way as their families. Or they might imitate the spending habits of influential people in their circle. Self-aware people differentiate their needs and expectations from those of others and are better able to withstand outside spending pressures. While open to advice and learning from outside your immediate circle, rely on your own judgment and resources when it comes to your spending.

• Relish the journey

People who are more self-aware find ways to reward themselves on their journey, even if only in small ways. Knowing what pleases you allows you to treat yourself along the way, in turn motivating you to keep going toward larger goals. Whatever your income level, make the most of it by identifying what gives you the most satisfaction for the buck.

• Avoid the keeping-up-with-the-Joneses syndrome

People who live in a state of gratitude are less likely to fall into a cycle of never-ending purchases that bring diminished periods of satisfaction. A dissatisfied person tends to try to keep up with the Joneses—rushing into purchases with the hope that their feelings will change when they buy the latest, shiniest object. Grateful people, on the other hand, take their time and look for just the right purchase.

EI Exercise:

If you are unable to afford what you want, substitute something less expensive that will still give some satisfaction. It is never all-or-nothing, so be flexible in finding affordable ways to reward yourself.

TIP 87

Become a great storyteller

"If a story is not about the hearer he [or she] will not listen . . . A great lasting story is about everyone or it will not last. The strange and foreign is not interesting—only the deeply personal and familiar." —John Steinbeck, 1962 Nobel Prize in Literature winner, from East of Eden

People have always been fascinated by stories. The first cave paintings from 27,000 years ago serve as an early form of storytelling. Stories told around a fire served as the first and only way to share dreams, entertain, inspire, and connect with others. Effective communication has always been about storytelling. Scientific evidence even backs up that good storytelling beats other forms of communication hands down. When we receive information from a PowerPoint presentation, we activate the part of our brain that decodes words into meaning. However, when we *listen* to a story, a lot more happens. In addition to the language-processing part of our brain, other parts begin to process the experience of the story for ourselves. An effective leader uses storytelling to share information and feelings while connecting with the people around him or her. Here are some elements of good storytelling to keep in mind.

• Keep it simple

Less is more; this is a basic rule of good storytelling. Avoid the complex and detailed, including the use of adjectives and complicated nouns. Using simple language is the best way to activate regions of the brain that help us relate to the events in a story. Remember that you are not trying to impress; you are trying to share an experience.

• Always keep the audience in mind

To be effective, the audience must be able to relate to the story. Talking about an experience on a yacht would not be a good way for the CEO of an organization to connect with frontline workers. This would likely have the opposite effect—distancing the audience from him or her. Telling a heartfelt story about going fishing with a family member or a grandchild would be much more effective.

• Share something of yourself

Talking too much about ourselves directly can be viewed by others as self-serving and turn them off. Skillful storytellers weave in information about themselves without appearing to be pretentious. Past stories of struggles and failures and about overcoming barriers are excellent sources for stories that help connect with the audience. The storyteller will appear more human, more like one of the audience members.

- **Share sincerely felt emotions**

If strong emotions arise when you're telling a story, consider expressing them. Showing some emotion increases trust and forms a bond between the speaker and the audience.

EI Exercise:

Don't take yourself too seriously. Audiences love speakers who are able to laugh at themselves. Let yourself be vulnerable. Share something downright embarrassing and silly. These moments will resonate strongly with the audience.

Show up strong in the first week of your dream job

"A new job is like a blank book, and you are the author." —Unknown

You've finally done it—landed the job you were after! All the hard work and preparation in getting the résumé and interview right have paid off. You are excited to start work and impress your new employer and get off on the right foot with your new coworkers. The first week of work can be exciting but also stressful. You're not quite sure how to dress and act so you make a great first impression. You have been told to just relax and be yourself, but you wonder if there are certain things you should be focused on during this crucial first week. Keep these things in mind.

- **Arrive early and stay late**

This will show enthusiasm for your job and leave a good impression. It's possible that your boss starts earlier than everyone else, but you should make a point that your coworkers see you there when they arrive at work. It's also a good idea to stay until others have gone home. Even though your workday may end at 5:30

p.m., it would not look good for you to be seen heading out the door at that time if your colleagues are still at their desks. While schedules and time spent at work may be very flexible, you want to play it safe your first week.

• Take the initiative and introduce yourself

Many workplaces will take you on a tour to introduce you to your colleagues. If that doesn't happen, go around and introduce yourself. Even if some employees have come around to introduce themselves to you, don't wait for everyone to do so. This indicates that you are someone who takes initiative.

• Ask good questions

You want to appear eager to learn and start contributing as soon as possible. One way to show interest is to prepare thoughtful questions to ask your boss and colleagues. Writing the answers down in a notebook or pad is a good way to show that you are serious about learning and not feigning an interest to make a good impression.

• Prepare to answer questions about yourself and your new job

Think about how you will answer questions concerning your previous work, putting your work history in a succinct and positive light. Even if your past job was not ideal, don't complain or make negative comments. Let your boss and colleagues know you are excited about your new job and want to contribute as soon as possible. Your colleagues may not all be familiar with your new role in the organization, so think of how you will answer this question.

- **Smile, relax, and offer to help whenever possible**

A simple smile goes a long way toward making a good first impression. Relax and be yourself . . . without looking *too* relaxed, such as leaning on the water cooler with your coffee mug while sharing jokes with your coworkers for extended periods. Offer to help whenever the opportunity arises. Extend that offer to your colleagues as well as your new boss—you want to avoid being seen as someone only interested in getting promoted as soon as possible.

EI Exercise:

Overdress a bit the first week of your new job. It shows self-respect and a positive attitude toward your new workplace. As you settle into your job, you will gain a sense of how people dress and you can adapt accordingly.

Handle criticism in a healthy way

"There is only one way to avoid criticism: do nothing, say nothing, and be nothing." —often attributed to Elbert Hubbard, writer and philosopher, in Little Journeys to the Homes of the Great, *Vol. 3*

Many situations trigger our fight or flight response. One such situation arises when we receive criticism. Our response might vary according to who delivers the criticism and how much power we perceive that person to have. The more power we perceive, the more likely we will feel a strong flight response. The fight response will also be stronger if we believe that the criticism is unjustified or unfair. But neither fight nor flight serves us well when criticized. When criticized—whether you believe you deserve the criticism or not—these techniques can help you make the most of a situation.

● **Prepare yourself**

Chances are you have received negative feedback at work at some point. How did you feel and react? If you had a chance to do it over again, would you handle the situation differently? In your mind, replay the scenario in a way that would result in the outcome you wanted. If it helps, role-play with a trusted friend, colleague, or family member. Come up with some responses that would help keep you on track—responses you could call up in future situations. Come up with a word, sound, phrase, or song that will remind you of the ideal situation you envisioned, and repeat it whenever the situation comes up again.

• Wait out strong emotions

If you're someone who interprets negative feedback as a verbal attack, you might experience powerful emotions that cause you to react before your "thinking brain" kicks in. The good news is that these strong emotions will quickly subside as your rational brain takes over. If you feel these strong emotions coming on, take a couple of deep breaths or do whatever you can to distract yourself. If the emotions are still highly volatile, ask for a time out and tell the person you will get back to him or her once you've had a chance to collect your thoughts. This gives you a chance to respond, rather than react.

• Repeat what you heard

A great way to start your response is to repeat, in your own words, what you heard the other person say. That individual might be expecting some pushback, perhaps anger or denial. By simply repeating what you thought was communicated, you diffuse any defensiveness and make the person more open to your feedback. When you give feedback, you are not taking blame or apologizing. You are simply making sure that you understand what the person is saying.

- **Engage and negotiate respectfully**

If you disagree with criticism, you can still create a win-win situation. Acknowledge that the one confronting you may feel that way, even though you hold a different view. In doing so, you move the conversation away from "let's prove right or wrong" to a place where real progress is possible. If you agree with the criticism, thank the individual for bringing it to your attention; admit that knowing this will help you in the future. If you don't agree, then agree to disagree, suggest other ways to resolve the issue, or ask for input from others.

EI Exercise:

Overcome your natural urge to defend yourself and just listen. Doing so invites the other party to feel less defensive and more willing to share information he or she might otherwise withhold. It also makes the person more open to hearing your side of the story.

TIP 90

Get serious about play at work

"You can discover more about a person in an hour of play than in a year of conversation."
—often attributed to Plato, Greek philosopher

It's time to get serious about bringing play into your workplace. Many see play as the opposite of work, something to do in your free time—a hobby or other form of rest and relaxation. However, incorporating play into your working environment actually holds substantial benefits that can make your work hours more relaxing, pleasurable, and more productive. The organization Playworks helps children develop healthy emotional and social skills through play. Playworks also helps companies incorporate play at work. According to Playworks, "the goal is inclusion, to remind everyone that we all are working toward the same goals, that we all have talents to bring to the workplace." Organizations like Google, LinkedIn, and Ideo recognize the benefits that play brings to their companies and have incorporated fun activities into their work environment. Here are compelling reasons your organization needs to get serious about play.

- **Reduces workplace stress**

Business leaders have long recognized that employees need to take regular breaks from intense activities to allow them to recharge. Throwing fun activities into the mix further helps us decompress. Play acts as a release valve for stress by taking our minds off upcoming deadlines and other pressures. We can then return to our duties refreshed and energized.

- **Increases teamwork**

Engaging in a playful activity as a team (when outcomes don't really matter) reminds us of the value of teamwork when outcomes *do* matter. These activities help each person focus on and appreciate the inputs of others and remind us that there is only so much we can do on our own; to be successful, we need to work together toward a common goal.

- **Builds better relationships**

As Plato stated, play can teach us a great deal about other people. Interacting with others in a fun, stress-free environment encourages increased openness and sharing. This in turn builds bonds that carry over into our work. Play allows staff to put aside, for a brief period, all the fences that are put up at work. By letting their guard down with each other, people gain new insights. This allows staff to better understand and relate to each other, and builds bridges between different levels of authority at work.

- **Builds emotional intelligence**

Playful environments allow people to express and manage emotions in a way they may not feel able to during the regular course of a working day. Employees might learn more about themselves and experiment with new ways of interacting in this safe, non-threatening setting.

- **Builds leadership skills**

Play is an excellent and safe way people can step out of their comfort zones and try on new leadership skills without the demands that such a role typically brings. Allowing everyone the option to take the lead in a natural play activity opens the door for discovering leadership potential that may otherwise have remained dormant.

EI Exercise:

Find a game to play at work—search the Internet for "team-building games at work" or go to teambuilding.com. Suggestions include team-building bingo, pub-like trivia, and guess the baby, as well as online office games.

Hang out with people different from you

"When everyone is thinking the same, no one is thinking."
—John Wooden, American basketball coach

We like to spend time with people who are like us. These people agree with us, think like us, and hold a similar viewpoint on issues. Yet only spending time with people like us keeps us in our comfort zone—and growth *occurs* outside our comfort zone. Spending time with people who are different from you might feel less comfortable, but that activity will . . .

- **Increase your self-awareness and acceptance of others**

Being around those who think differently from you helps you understand yourself better. You become more conscious of the reasons you chose to be and think as you do, and you thus escape the trap of believing there is only one way to see things. This practice helps keep you out of us-versus-them and right-versus-wrong thinking patterns. Instead of black and white, you see a lot of gray.

- **Challenge you to think critically**

People who are different challenge your ways of thinking, your perceptions, and your norms. They make you aware that many perspectives exist, each supported by its own logic. This awareness will challenge you to change your own perceptions if you find others that make more sense.

- **Allow you to benefit from the strengths of others**

All of us have strengths and weaknesses. For example, someone may be a big-picture thinker with little interest and patience in the details. This person would greatly benefit from including a detail person in his or her close circle, to help consider all the consequences of a particular action. The reverse benefit would come to the detail person, who might find it difficult to make decisions because he or she gets bogged down in the details.

- **Help you make better decisions**

When your circle of relationships includes people who see situations from many different angles, you gain a more complete picture, which helps you make more informed decisions. Abraham Lincoln was well-known for appointing people to his cabinet who thought quite differently from him. While many would find this threatening, he realized that he had blind spots in his own thinking and needed people who were strong in the areas where he was weak. This helped him form a strong, multi-faceted team that was seldom caught off guard.

- **Add zest and imagination to life**

While being around those like us can make us comfortable, it can also cause us to become boring, unimaginative, and dull. We need challenge in our lives to keep us sharp and stimulated. Hanging out with people of different backgrounds and worldviews opens up a whole new and exciting world of possibilities for us to imagine and have fun with.

EI Exercise:

You can get a preview of different-thinking people—right now—by reading up on various cultures, religions, or countries. Or meet others in person by volunteering with refugee-relief organizations. Consider mentoring or hosting those displaced by war.

TIP 92

Boost your emotional intelligence every day

*"Sow a thought, and you reap an act; sow an act,
and you reap a habit; sow a habit, and you reap a character;
sow a character, and you reap a destiny."*
*—attributed to Samuel Smiles, author and government
reformer, from* Happy Homes and the Hearts That Make Them

Much of what's written about emotional intelligence implies that a large amount of ongoing effort and a lifetime commitment is required. Understandably, some people may find that idea overwhelming. While any type of change can involve commitment and effort over a long period of time, there are simple actions you can take that will yield immediate results. Incorporate these actions into your daily routine. After seeing the benefits of doing a few basic things differently, you may want to go deeper into developing your emotional intelligence.

- **Become more aware of your feelings**

Check your feelings a few times a day and pay attention to them, rather than relegate them to the background. Stand outside of yourself as an observer. This increases awareness of your feelings and gives you more control. Since emotional intelligence is about managing your feelings, becoming more aware of them is a crucial first step. Look for an opportunity each day to share at least one positive emotion. Perhaps start by letting someone know that what they did or said lifted you up.

- **Become a better listener**

Emotional intelligence is about building stronger connections with others. You can do this by becoming a better listener. In one conversation today, repeat in your own words what you heard. Ask questions. You will gain a level of respect in the other person's eyes, even if you don't completely agree with each other.

- **Avoid monologues and work on conversations**

We all know people who ramble on about something solely of interest to them. They seem oblivious to the fact that we may not be interested. When *you* initiate conversation, ask yourself if the topic you are excited about will also be interesting to the listeners. Better yet, ask your listeners about themselves. Practice doing so on a daily basis. Most people love to talk about themselves. Also, remember details about people that are important to them and bring them up in a future conversation. This will forge deeper connection.

- Give yourself a brief time out when experiencing strong negative emotions

Road rage is an example of anger running amuck. Powerful emotions like that will subside, however, if we don't immediately act on them. If you feel anger rising, it's time to pause. Take some deep breaths or remove yourself from the situation until you feel calmer. Similarly, practice noticing when *any* strong emotion rises within you; step back and look at it objectively, considering its source and if you need to act on it or can simply acknowledge it.

EI Exercise:

Before you go to sleep, briefly look over your interactions that day. What went well and what could have gone better? If you tried something different and it worked better, enjoy the feeling of knowing that you are in charge of your feelings and actions. If something didn't go well, think of how you might have handled it differently. Resolve to try something else next time.

TIP 93

Adapt to your rapidly changing workplace

"Vulnerability is not weakness, and the uncertainty, risk, and emotional exposure we face every day are not optional. Our only choice is a question of engagement. Our willingness to own and engage with our vulnerability determines the depth of our courage and the clarity of our purpose; the level to which we protect ourselves from being vulnerable is a measure of our fear and disconnection." —Brené Brown, author of Daring Greatly

Technological advances are altering how we work, live, and think. Due to artificial intelligence—and the capability of algorithms to pull together massive amounts of information quickly and accurately—virtually all fields risk some disruption from automation. Both employees and management realize that the degree of adjustment will only increase. Add to that the realities of market dynamics, social media, globalization, and diversity. Whether you are at the entry level in an organization or the CEO, all roles will require a high level of ability to cope effectively with the pace of change. Consider these steps to boost your adaptability.

- **Overcome falling into the familiar and comfortable**

Our default position, when confronted with change, is to fall back into our comfort zone. As an emotionally intelligent person, you'll recognize that this is happening and work to overcome this urge to stay with the tried and true. Your awareness of your own behavior patterns and emotional drivers gives you a real advantage in dealing with altering variables and an expanse of uncharted territory.

- **Turn emotions into allies**

Change brings up emotions from both ends of the emotional spectrum: excitement and anxiety. Become aware of the emotion. As an emotionally intelligent person, you possess the ability to turn that emotion into an ally and gain an edge in moving through a major disruption.

- **Seek out diverse opinions and perspectives**

Be aware that your perspective, knowledge, and beliefs have limitations. Allow yourself to be more accepting of ideas that are new or even contrary to what you have believed in the past. This openness opens you to new and untried initiatives and a willingness to take risks—a necessary trait that will become increasingly important, allowing you to thrive and stay relevant in the new economy.

- **Cut to the chase quickly**

In any change, people's internal resistance can sabotage the change process if not uncovered and dealt with. People may want to be seen as open to change but often have underlying reasons to resist. Emotionally intelligent people can often discern others' feelings and thus gain insight into the resistance. This awareness facilitates communication. Their awareness of verbal nuances and nonverbal cues allows them to home in and address what's below the surface—increasing the likelihood that resistant employees will accept the new direction or changes that are being considered.

EI Exercise:

The next time you're confronted with an uncomfortable emotion, practice reappraisal: change the way you view the emotion. For example, instead of feeling anxiety over a work mistake, think of it instead as a learning experience.

TIP 94

Take charge when you feel unappreciated at work

"We spend too much valuable time at work so it is important to feel engaged in our work and not report to work out of habit or routine. If work is not intentional, we suffer along with our company." —Judy Bell, president of Judy Bell Consulting

Most of us, at some point in our working lives, have felt unappreciated. Feeling undervalued leads to a loss for yourself as well as the organization. For you, the results could be increased negativity, or loss of motivation or morale. For the organization, that adds up to a loss of productivity. We also know that feeling unappreciated leads to increased stress and anxiety. Not feeling valued in the workplace has negative impact on your health both at work and at home. If you feel unappreciated, take initiative and look for ways to turn things around, starting with these steps.

- **Check out your perceptions**

Find someone who knows the quality of your work as well as what your organization considers good work—a trusted colleague or a respected manager to whom you don't report. Don't get caught up in a cycle of negativity and only talk to coworkers known to be chronic complainers. Instead, talk to people who appear upbeat and positive. And don't make assumptions about your boss and what you perceive as his or her lack of appreciation. Your boss may be unaware of the excellent work you are doing or may be under great pressure. Start with that assumption and go with it until you have evidence to prove it wrong.

- **Request a conversation with your boss**

In this case, you need to be subtle. Prepare for the meeting beforehand by knowing what you are going to discuss and preparing a list of recent accomplishments. Never say you want more appreciation; rather, indicate that there are times you don't feel that your work is noticed. If you are part of a team, mention the work of the team instead of focusing on your own achievements. Avoid confronting your boss or going in to speak when you are angry. That will only put your boss on the defensive. Rather, ask for feedback on your performance. Indicate to your boss that you are looking for ways to improve and would like his or her help.

- **Recognize the contributions of others**

Give credit to the team when you get a win. In front of your boss and peers, praise others who have done a good job—even down to who created your professional reports and presentations. This will create awareness of the need for appreciation, and there is a good chance that the recognition of a job well done will be reciprocated. Make sure your appreciation is genuine; when unwarranted appreciation is loosely tossed around, real appreciation quickly loses its effectiveness and value.

- **Look for what went well**

Many of us tend to focus on what went wrong. Even if five of six reports we created received praise, we will focus on the one that received critical feedback. Instead, try to look for what went well at the end of each day, each week, each month. Make a list and post it where you can easily see it. Not only will this list give you a boost, but it will also increase your ability to notice the positive instead of just the negative. As you intrinsically motivate yourself, you won't have to wait for outside validation. Remember: real fulfilment and satisfaction come from within.

- **Consider the alternatives**

What if the bigger problem in you not being appreciated stems from a bad boss and a toxic work culture? Are the benefits of staying where you won't be appreciated worth it? Can you self-motivate and continue, or do you need to move on for the sake of your mental health, well-being, and self-respect?

EI Exercise:

Whether you're a team member or team leader, after the successful completion of a project, surprise everyone by bringing in bagels and cream cheese (or doughnuts) for everyone. Drop by your supervisor's office and let him or her know the treats are available.

TIP 95

Do this when facing adversity

*"But I have found that in the simple act of living with hope,
and in the daily effort to have a positive impact in the world,
the days I do have are made all the more meaningful
and precious. And for that I am grateful."*
—Elizabeth Edwards, attorney, author, and health-care advocate

Have you ever had one of those days where one thing after another goes wrong, and then someone comes along and tells you to stay positive? You feel like strangling that person on the spot. Regardless of those feelings, don't simply host your own pity party. Engage in these actions to help you move on.

● Step away and get a reality check

When we are in a negative state, we tend to see problems as greater than they are and overreact. Ask yourself: "Is there anything I can do at this time to keep the problem from getting worse?" Or even: "How could this problem have been worse than it is?" This may help you see some light at the end of the tunnel. Or if you're still stuck in negativity, ask someone you trust to offer his or her perspective.

- **Look for a positive and focus on it**

When you have just learned some bad news, it will not be easy to focus on something positive. Try to shift your thinking, however, to another situation that went well or to something that has brought you joy and happiness. Or even think of something neutral. Do whatever it takes to shift your focus. And consider the long game: the life stories of most highly successful people include at least one chapter on overcoming tragedies and failures. Nietzsche said, "What doesn't kill us will make us stronger." People who have survived adversity and gone on to better their lives believe this and look back on their difficult times with a sense of pride for having overcome them.

- **Look past the situation**

Think of difficult situations from your past. This one, too, will pass. Try to imagine what it will be like a year, five years, or ten years from now. This action will help you focus on doing the difficult work to get through *this* crisis, keeping it in perspective. After all, it's not the only thing happening in your life right now.

- **Ask for and accept help**

Successful people have built a strong support network. If you have such a network, this is the time to reach out and ask for help. Knowing when we need help and asking for it is a sign of strength, not of weakness. We feel good when we are able to help others, so let others experience that same feeling by being able to help you in times of need. If you don't have an immediate support network, or have recently moved to an area where you don't know anyone, reach out to organizations in your community whose purpose is to offer support.

EI Exercise:

If you don't have a support network, start developing one right away. Such networks don't happen by accident; they are built up over time with effort and consistency. Start by offering to help others in times of need. What we put out to others comes back to us multiplied. Who needs your help today?

TIP 96

Actively look for a mentor

While the majority of people believe that mentoring is important, only a small percentage have taken the time and effort to find a good mentor.

Mentoring serves an important function in developing growth and success. Research on mentoring has found that the greater the emotional intelligence of the mentor, the more the mentee will trust this person and the advice offered. Qualities we look for in an emotionally intelligent mentor include self-awareness, self-regulation, motivation, empathy, and social skills. Consider these other markers in a potential mentor, to determine if he or she is right for you.

- **Displays a high degree of self-awareness**

In talking to potential mentors, ask not only about their successes but also about their failures, their struggles, and their lessons learned. Mentors with a high degree of EI will openly share their feelings, fears, and doubts and what they did to overcome them. They will share their vulnerabilities—areas they are still working to overcome. Beware of someone who appears to have all the answers and is not open to sharing vulnerabilities.

- **Focuses on the needs of the mentee**

A high degree of self-confidence and a healthy ego are necessary for success, but when it comes to mentoring, the mentor's ego must take a back seat to the needs of the person being mentored. An emotionally intelligent mentor is secure in his or her own abilities and doesn't need ego-stroking. A secure person won't take credit for success but will instead heap praise upon his or her teams or partners. You will get the feeling that this person receives satisfaction from seeing others succeed.

- **Keeps a degree of detachment**

Mentorship with any depth and quality can become emotionally charged at times. The mentee may be making crucial decisions that will impact the rest of his or her life and so needs someone able to remain objective. When looking for a mentor, find out how this individual handled emotionally charged situations in the past and what he or she personally learned in the process. Was he able to control himself during an emotionally charged situation? Did she take a break until she could cool off?

- **Guides the mentee to come to his or her own decisions**

Good mentors offer guidance, support, and different perspectives but recognize that it is up to the mentee to ultimately make the decisions. After all, the mentee has to live with the consequences. Foram Sheth, chief coaching officer and cofounder of Ama La Vida, writes, "A good mentor will ask thought-provoking questions based on observation and active listening to help the mentee explore different possibilities, to uncover blind spots, and help the mentee move from problem to solution." Emotionally intelligent mentors also realize that what they would do is not necessarily what is best for the person they are mentoring. When considering a mentor, ask what you should do in a situation. If they help you probe deeper and further, consider them as a potential candidate. If they tell you directly what you should do, move on and look for someone else.

- **Demonstrates service, success, and a positive attitude**

Since mentorship is often a free service provided by the mentor, look for someone who genuinely enjoys helping others. The best mentors have a history of giving to their families, others, and their community because they feel a sense of responsibility to give back. While they may not be incredibly wealthy or successful in all areas of life, good mentors have experienced success in overcoming barriers in life. They openly express gratitude and have a positive, optimistic outlook toward the future. They take responsibility for their mistakes and shortcomings and feel proud of what they have accomplished. You get the feeling that they are able to relate to your struggles because they have been there themselves. Be careful of anyone who is still going through a difficult situation—this person may be looking for someone to commiserate with rather than to help.

EI Exercise:

Not sure of a mentor's service history? Bring up volunteer activities that you have done or plan to do, and see how they react. Highly emotionally intelligent mentors will be able to share how it makes them feel to help others.

TIP 97

Take these steps when your boss lacks emotional intelligence

"You always learn from both good and bad bosses."
—Rajeev Suri, Inmarsat CEO and former Nokia CEO

Bad bosses come in all shapes and sizes. Some are downright bullies, not caring if they lose their temper or hurt the feelings of those who report to them. Others are egotists who believe they are smarter than everyone else and have no need to listen to or take feedback from those they are supposed to serve. In between are the micromanagers, the ones who are unaware, unable to make decisions, or willing to take credit for your work and the work of others. The list is endless but the consequences are predictable: bad morale, greater turnover, decreased engagement, and loss of productivity. Unless we have been extremely fortunate or have limited work experience, chances are we have had one of these bosses in our working lives. The question is: "What do we do about it?" If you have compelling reasons to stick around and believe there is a possibility you can help your boss make some needed changes, here are actions you can pursue.

- **Try not to take it personally**

Chances are your boss is not deliberately setting out to make your life miserable. Try to have empathy and imagine what pressures he or she may be facing from superiors, or other factors that may be making life difficult. Giving your boss the benefit of the doubt will keep you from getting caught up in negative feelings and draining energy that could be used more productively.

- **Don't make assumptions about your boss's motivation or character**

Unless your boss has told you that he is aware of what he is doing, or that she outright doesn't care, don't assume that your boss *is* aware. Some people are simply blind to the effect they have on others—an example of low emotional intelligence.

- **Find out what motivates him or her**

People have the greatest motivation to change if that change would help them achieve what they're working toward. Do you know what keeps your boss up at night or brings the most stress? If you can discern these pressure points—and if it's appropriate to offer help—you might build rapport and a relationship. Your only hope of influencing your boss will be to get yourself in a place where he or she trusts you and sees value in what you are offering.

- **Demonstrate what you would like more of from your boss**

Do trusted colleagues have any insights on how to improve your relationship with your boss? If your boss's poor behavior extends to others, not just you, consider how your team might model how they'd prefer to be treated. At staff meetings, encourage people to praise each other and show appreciation for others' efforts. In front of your boss, give colleagues credit for a job well done. If your boss lacks empathy, make a point of showing empathy to others in the organization who have suffered through illness or loss. Share books and articles on emotional intelligence, and suggest speakers for upcoming conferences or staff development. Talk about people your boss looks up to in terms of their high emotional intelligence.

EI Exercise:

Catch your boss doing something positive, something you appreciate, and let him or her know. If you see any changes toward the better, let your boss know that it was noticed and appreciated.

TIP 98

Make the most of a nasty boss

"Having a bad boss isn't your fault. Staying with one is."
—Nora Denzl, AMD lead independent director

Bad bosses can make your life a living hell. We're talking about more than someone who is merely disorganized, incompetent, or absent but still a decent person. What do you do if your boss is narcissistic, bullying, arrogant, and backstabbing, or takes credit for your work? Heed these ideas.

- **Work on your escape plan**

You need to get out before all of your emotional energy is sucked out of you. Consider what you need to do, not only to keep your sanity but also to develop your skills—using your current job to get to the next level. This calls for some strategic thinking. Find ways to work around your boss and cope with his or her behavior until you are out of there. Admittedly, you are in a disadvantaged position. Going above your boss or directly to human resources is usually not a good idea because HR serves the needs of the company, not individual employees. HR is likely to encourage you to talk with your boss about your concerns, or will relay your concerns *to* your boss, which can make your life difficult.

- **Look for allies and support from other areas**

Don't go around complaining about your boss to anyone at work. It will waste your energy and could make the situation worse. Help out your colleagues whenever you can and build a supportive workplace environment. Find opportunities to work in areas outside of your own and build relationships with others on your boss's level—those who might give you a positive reference when you move on. Also, building good working relationships with coworkers will help diffuse some of the negative energy while you are still there.

- **Find ways to influence and manage his or her behavior**

Most of what influences us works on a subconscious level. So if you're not able to walk away from your job quite yet, you want your boss to perceive you as an ally. This could change how he or she treats you, even subtly. So do some intelligence gathering. What impresses or influences your boss? Whom does she admire? What are his favorite ways of getting things done? What are her belief systems—what does she value in life? Find ways to use this knowledge to your advantage. If your boss admires someone in the organization, subtly slip in a positive reference to that person when an opportunity arises. If he or she strongly believes in family values, slip in references to the strong family values you were raised with.

- **Don't cower, but don't get into a power struggle**

To keep your dignity intact, you might have to let your boss know that what he or she does bothers you. Some individuals only respect people who have the courage to stand up to them, and your boss may be one of these. But keep in mind: if you find yourself in a power struggle, you will lose. Never confront your boss when you are emotionally charged; wait until you are calm and collected. In an interaction, the person able to keep his or her emotions under control comes out looking the best. Do not attack and accuse your boss of actions; rather, speak about the impact of your boss's actions on you. Make "I" statements. For example: "I felt attacked and embarrassed in front of my coworkers when you yelled at me in the staff meeting."

- **Give your best and manage your emotions**

It is not easy to do your best and keep your emotions in check when you might be criticized and when your work is not valued. Think of yourself as working for yourself, instead of your boss or the organization. Any skills you learn will make you a more valued person for your new employer. Use your present job to develop yourself, not only your skills but also your coping mechanisms. Surviving, and even thriving, through a nasty boss experience will heighten your appreciation of a good boss. More important than anyone else recognizing your strengths and abilities is that *you* recognize them. Giving your best, regardless of those around you, will increase your sense of self-worth and self-confidence. That is really your ultimate goal.

EI Exercise:

Update your résumé and start (or keep adding) to your "kudos" file—compliments from coworkers as well as awards and other recognitions.

TIP 99

Work to become more empathetic

"The great gift of human beings is that we have the power of empathy." —Meryl Streep, Academy Award–winning actress

From the boardroom to the classroom, *empathy* is a word we are hearing more and more. According to biologist Frans de Waal in his book *The Age of Empathy*, we are social creatures who have naturally evolved to take care of each other. While empathy develops early, we also know that we can increase it throughout our lifetime. And perhaps no other attribute is more vital to developing relationships with others. Here are ways you can increase your empathy.

- **Focus on what the other person is saying**

Empathy requires that we cultivate the trait of active listening—being totally focused on what the other person is saying. To practice this, pretend that your job is to listen closely to someone so you can accurately feed back to them the conversation. A bonus: by listening carefully, you'll receive additional information and can encourage that person to go deeper into the conversation. As your active listening skills increase, you will find people drawn to you and opening up to you more.

- ## Challenge prejudices and stereotypes

To learn and grow we need to push ourselves into new territory. One way to do this: make an effort to know people who are *not like you*. Find someone you might be somewhat uncomfortable around because of those differences, and make a genuine attempt to get to know him or her. Uncover common struggles and joys. Ask questions to learn why they believe and think the way they do. Attend events where the crowd is different from those you normally hang out with.

- ## Develop a curiosity about others

Have you ever wondered about the unhoused person panhandling across the street from where you work? Have you asked yourself how he came to that situation, if she has family or friends, or how he views the world? What about the person who cleans your office—ever wondered about his or her dreams, goals, and aspirations? Many people are curious, but few take the time to step out of their comfort zone to ask. Challenge yourself to slowly find out more. You may be surprised by what you learn.

- ## Spend some time in another's shoes

George Orwell worked as a colonial policeman in Burma when he decided to find out what it was like to live as a beggar and vagabond. He dressed like a tramp and lived on the streets of London with the rest of the homeless. For Orwell, it was a life-changing experience, providing great literary material and a fresh perspective on living. He considered this to be the most valuable experience of his life. For more than ten years, New York Yankees general manager Brian Cashman and hundreds of others have voluntarily slept one night on the streets of Manhattan in freezing or near-freezing temperatures to raise awareness about homeless children. There are other ways to experience how people live, such as spending a month surviving on what someone receives on welfare or volunteering with those who are marginalized.

EI Exercise:

Share yourself with others. This does not mean spilling your whole life story within five minutes of meeting someone. But share some of your fears as well as your joys and aspirations. By doing so, you give others permission to share more of themselves, allowing for deeper conversation.

TIP 100

Boost your emotional toughness

"Keeping your body healthy increases your resilience, making it easier to dismiss criticism and self-doubt." —Dr. Betsy Holmberg, psychologist and writer for Psychology Today

We may think the world takes advantage of kind, caring, empathic people because they lack the ability to be emotionally tough. Emotional toughness, however, does not require us to be belligerent, stoic, or unconcerned with what others feel or think. It just involves standing up for what we believe in and setting firm boundaries. As with any other skill, you can develop emotional toughness. Try these steps.

- **Trust your judgment**

"Fool me once, shame on you; fool me twice, shame on me." Listen to your gut if you feel concern over trusting someone or some situation. You may make mistakes, but as you learn from those mistakes, you'll gradually hone your instincts. Emotionally tough people have learned how to trust that inner voice.

- **Continually push through your comfort zones**

By continually taking action that falls outside your comfort zone, you expand those boundaries. Your enlarged comfort zone leads to a willingness to take on more challenges, bringing you ever closer to reaching your potential and less likely to let naysayers sway you from your goals.

- **Practice self-discipline**

Draw on your inner persistence and determination to boost yourself both physically and mentally. Get enough sleep, stick to an exercise schedule, and take the time and effort to eat healthy food. Even when you don't feel like following your schedule, remind yourself how good it will feel when you do.

- **Choose to associate with positive people**

While you can't choose your family or the environment you grew up in, you can choose the people you want around you. People who become emotionally strong commit themselves to finding and maintaining strong relationships with people who are growing, striving, and moving toward their goals. As you support people who inspire you, they will support you, in turn, on your own journey.

- **Strive toward your goals without comparing yourself to others**

Emotionally strong people don't get caught up in wondering how they stack up to others, or how others see them. "We have two thought networks: the one that cares about what other people think, and the one that focuses on goals," explains psychologist Betsy Holmberg. "By attending to their goals, emotionally tough people turn off the judgmental, doubtful part of their brains."

Keep in mind that you have a larger goal and purpose that you strive toward.

El Exercise:

Do an everyday thing differently. Dr. Oliver Page, contributor to PositivePsychology.com, writes, "In everyday life, there are ample opportunities to challenge yourself. Turn off your smartphone and television while having dinner, decide what to wear more quickly, or just slow down to take in the surroundings on a walk. These changes break you out of old, comfortable routines."

TIP 101

Maintain your determination

"Enclose your heart in times of need with the steel of your determination and your strength. In doing this, all things will be bearable." —Lora Leigh, author of Broken Wings

In every success story, the longest chapter is the one on determination. While success demands many things from us, willpower and determination always rise to the top of the list. Many people believe that we are born with determination and that those who succeed are simply the fortunate ones born with an abundant supply. However, ask successful people, and they will tell you how they could always find a way to harness and use what they had more effectively. Here are ways to harness your determination.

- **Set up your day the night before**

Before you go to sleep, make some basic decisions about the next day, such as what you will wear and what you will eat for lunch, as well as the route you will take to work. Pack a healthy lunch the night before rather than find yourself forced to purchase from the hot dog vendor. The same applies to spending money: decide on a budget and stick to it. Also, decide the night before that you won't check your email or surf the net before you have finished the more important tasks. Stick to your schedule, and at the end of the day close your eyes for a few minutes and take in how good you feel to be in charge of your day. Getting into the habit of planning your day in advance will take the routine decisions off the table, making it easier to avoid getting sidetracked and wasting time and energy on unimportant things.

• Do the most difficult things first

The most difficult duties will not get easier the more you put them off. You will only waste energy that would be better spent by just digging in. Get after the hardest job right away while you are still fresh. Research has shown that our minds are sharpest in the morning, so that's when you should tackle the tough jobs. Then, relax and take care of the more routine to-dos. Becoming disciplined and getting the hard jobs done sooner rather than later gives a sense of satisfaction and frees up energy you might otherwise spend in worrying.

• Eliminate distractions and time wasters

Real emergencies come up and have to be dealt with. However, the majority of what we face do not constitute true emergencies; many will resolve themselves on their own. When you are working on a difficult task, you might be tempted to jump to a request that pops up, especially one that is easier. Immediately responding to these requests will only set you up to receive more. By not responding, you convey that you are a focused person who is busy.

Over time you will be bothered less by trivial, time-wasting matters. Successful people stay focused on the most important work until it is completed.

● **Regenerate and keep up your energy**

If you're working on something but feel your energy or ideas fading, take a quick break: walk, run, stretch, or do whatever regenerates your energy. You will return to your task with renewed vigor and a sharper mental focus. Instead of eating a large meal at lunch, snack on healthy food such as fresh fruit and vegetables during the day. Drink plenty of water and get into a regular exercise program. Arrange a routine with these matters so that they just become part of your daily regime.

EI Exercise:

Create a vision board that serves as a constant reminder of your ultimate goals. Or create a mind movie or another system that reminds you of the "why" behind the goal. For example, if you want to earn enough money to start a school in a developing nation, create a clear vision of what the school would look like. Set aside regular time daily, if only five minutes, to visualize this goal. The more details you can put in, the better.

Acknowledgments

Firstly, I would like to acknowledge my late mother, Helene Deutschendorf, who always sacrificed, believed in, and supported me despite difficult circumstances in her own life. Her unselfish, kind, and caring nature brought light to a world that had too often been dark for her. Also, a huge thank you to Sandra for always believing in me, coming up with great ideas, and excellent editing.

Even a few timely powerful words from the right person can have a powerful impact on our lives. My high school principal, Robert McDonald, spoke such words to me at a time when they were desperately needed. They provided me with inspiration to carry on and believe that I could achieve whatever I wanted in life.

I would like to thank Joshua Freedman, whose work with Six Seconds has been a great resource and inspiration for me. Next I would like to thank Daniel Goleman, whose ground-breaking work on Emotional Intelligence brought it into the public sphere. His first book, *Emotional Intelligence: Why it can matter more than IQ*, inspired me to learn as much as I could about EQ and make it my mission to spread the word through my teaching and writing. Thank you to Dr. Reuven Bar-On who developed the first scientific assessment tool for emotional intelligence. It is through learning about and using this tool that gave started my EI journey. Along the route I credit Dr. Steven Stein and David Cory that were instrumental in my continuing efforts to expand my knowledge of emotional intelligence.

I would like to thank all the wonderful editors I have worked with in the Life/Work Section of Fast Company. Their challenges, support, and belief in me inspired me to continually work on elevating my writing skills.

This book would never have seen the light of day had it not been for the dedication and perseverance of my agent, John Willig. It has been a real pleasure working with him. Thank you also to all the people at Dexterity Publishing for seeing the value in my writing and for your efforts in making this book a reality.

Thank you to my editor, Morgan Rickey, for her keen eye to detail, positive warm support and knowing just the right words to cut as well as to add.

Lastly, but certainly not least, I credit the Mankind Project (MKP) with providing a safe place and support for me to learn more about myself and how my emotions impact me. I can't say enough about how much this group of special men has given to help themselves and other men live more whole, fulfilling lives. A special thanks to the men of the MKP Edmonton Community for their ongoing support and for challenging me to be a better man.

About the Author

Harvey Deutschendorf is an emotional intelligence expert, TEDx speaker, and published author of *The Other Kind of Smart: Simple Ways to Boost Your Emotional Intelligence for Greater Personal Effectiveness and Success*. Harvey has been published in various publications such as *Turkish Airlines Magazine*, *Toronto Star*, *Toastmasters International*, *Reader's Digest*, *Forbes*, *Carrier Management*, *Silicon Republic*, *Well Being World* and is a regular contibutor to *Fast Company* and *HRProfessionalsMagazine*.

Connect with Harvey at https://www.theotherkindofsmart.com/ and take his Emotional Intelligence Quiz to see how you rank on the emotional intelligence scale at https://www.theotherkindofsmart.com/ei-quiz

If you enjoyed this book please leave a review wherever books are sold.